COLLECTIVE INVESTMENT SCHEME TRANSACTIONS IN ASEAN+3

BENCHMARK PRODUCT AND MARKET INFRASTRUCTURE DESIGN

SEPTEMBER 2022

ASIAN DEVELOPMENT BANK

ADB

Notes:
ADB recognizes "China" as the People's Republic of China; "Hong Kong" as Hong Kong, China; "Korea" as the Republic of Korea; and "Vietnam" as Viet Nam.

In this report, international standards for naming conventions—International Organization for Standardization (ISO) 3166 for economy codes and ISO 4217 for currency codes—are used to reflect the discussions of the Cross-Border Settlement Infrastructure Forum to improve cross-border bond and cash settlement infrastructures in the region. ASEAN+3 comprises the Association of Southeast Asian Nations (ASEAN) plus the People's Republic of China, Japan, and the Republic of Korea.

The economies of ASEAN+3 as defined in ISO 3166 include Brunei Darussalam (BN; BRN); Cambodia (KH; KHM); the People's Republic of China (CN; CHN); Hong Kong, China (HK; HKG); Indonesia (ID; IDN); Japan (JP; JPN); the Republic of Korea (KR; KOR); the Lao People's Democratic Republic (LA; LAO); Malaysia (MY; MYS); Myanmar (MM; MMR); the Philippines (PH; PHL); Singapore (SG; SGP); Thailand (TH; THA); and Viet Nam (VN; VNM).

The currencies of ASEAN+3 as defined in ISO 4217 include the Brunei dollar (BND), Cambodian riel (KHR), Chinese yuan (CNY), Hong Kong dollar (HKD), Indonesian rupiah (IDR), Japanese yen (JPY), Korean won (KRW), Lao kip (LAK), Malaysian ringgit (MYR), Myanmar kyat (MMK), Philippine peso (PHP), Singapore dollar (SGD), Thai baht (THB), and Vietnamese dong (VND).

Cover design by Joseph Francis M. Manio.

CONTENTS

TABLES, FIGURES, AND BOXES

BOXES

STATEMENT FROM THE CROSS-BORDER SETTLEMENT INFRASTRUCTURE FORUM CHAIR

With 2022 in full swing, I would like to express our deepest appreciation, as the acting chair and vice-chair, to our members and observers for their unwavering support for the Cross-Border Settlement Infrastructure Forum (CSIF).

Since its inception in 2013, CSIF has facilitated dialogue on the promotion of intra-regional financial transactions. In 2014, CSIF officially proposed central securities depository and real-time gross settlement (CSD-RTGS) linkage as the most suitable delivery versus payment model for the Asian Bond Markets Initiative, based on the consensus of Association of Southeast Asian Nations plus the People's Republic of China, Japan, and the Republic of Korea (ASEAN+3) members. In July 2020, after a series of studies and discussions, CSIF unveiled its blueprint for future directions in a report titled *Next Steps for ASEAN+3 Central Securities Depository and Real-Time Gross Settlement Linkages*.

In 2021, as a next step in enhancing the post-trade efficiency of Asian bond markets, CSIF expanded its research focus to explore the feasibility of applying the CSD-RTGS delivery versus payment model to collective investment scheme (CIS) passports. Months of efforts have culminated in this report.

This document covers a wide range of topics including the European CIS passport (UCITS), the pan-European settlement engine (TARGET2-Securities), the Asian CIS passports (Asia Region Funds Passport and ASEAN CIS), CIS market intelligence in ASEAN+3, and other survey results.

This report is the product of collaborative research among Satoru Yamadera (CSIF Secretariat), Ki Hoon Ro (Specialist of the Korea Securities Depository), and many other seasoned consultants. We would like to extend our heartfelt gratitude to the Asian Development Bank for technical assistance and all the hardworking experts for drafting, revising, and editing this insightful document.

Seung-Kwon Lee
Acting Chair, CSIF
Vice-Chair, CSIF
Director, Clearing and Settlement Department
Korea Securities Depository

ACKNOWLEDGMENTS

As the Secretariat of the Cross-Border Settlement Infrastructure Forum (CSIF), the Asian Development Bank (ADB) would like to extend its profound gratitude to the chair, vice-chair, and other stakeholders of CSIF for their continuous support and guidance throughout the entire period of this study.

ADB is also grateful to CSIF members and observers for dedicating their time and efforts to advance this study. In particular, the two rounds of extensive surveys conducted would not have been possible without the timely and accurate responses of participants.

This study intends to examine the feasibility of applying a central securities depository and real-time gross settlement linkage model to collective investment scheme passports in Asia. The research objective is considered a constructive approach to enhancing the operational efficiency and global standing of the Asian financial infrastructure, which is compatible with ADB's commitment to drive infrastructure investments for sustainable economic growth in the region.

ADB will continue to work toward the betterment of member economies and the prosperity of Asia by promoting regional dialogue and pursuing new research topics.

ABBREVIATIONS

ABMI	Asian Bond Markets Initiative
ACMF	ASEAN Capital Markets Forum
AFSF	Asia Fund Standardization Forum
AIF	Alternative Investment Fund
AMBD	Monetary Authority of Brunei Darussalam
AML/KYC	anti-money laundering and know-your-client
ARFP	Asia Region Funds Passport
ASEAN	Association of Southeast Asian Nations
BETS	Book-Entry Transfer System
BIC	Business Identifier Code
BSP	Bangko Sentral ng Pilipinas
CDEP	Central Data Exchange Platform
CHATS	Clearing House Automated Transfer System
CIS	collective investment scheme
CMU	Central Moneymarkets Unit
CNY	Chinese yuan
CSD	central securities depository
CSD-RTGS	central securities depository and real-time gross settlement
CSDC	China Securities Depository and Clearing Corporation
CSDR	Central Securities Depository Regulation
CSIF	Cross-Border Settlement Infrastructure Forum
CSRC	China Securities Regulatory Commission
CSX	Cambodia Securities Exchange
DCA	dedicated cash account
DVP	delivery versus payment
EFAMA	Europe Fund and Asset Management Association
ETF	exchange-traded fund
FDEP	Financial Data Exchange Platform
FMI	financial market infrastructure
FORS	CMU Fund Order Routing and Settlement Service
FPSG	Fund Processing Standardization Group
HKD	Hong Kong dollar
HKMA	Hong Kong Monetary Authority
ICSD	international central securities depository
ISO	International Organization for Standardization
JASDEC	Japan Securities Depository Center
KSD	Korea Securities Depository

KSEI	PT Kustodian Sentral Efek Indonesia (Indonesia Central Securities Depository)
ManCo	management company
MRF	Mutual Recognition of Funds
NAV	net asset value
PRC	People's Republic of China
RTGS	real-time gross settlement
SEC	Securities and Exchange Commission
SME	securities maintaining entity
SMO	Securities Markets Order
SMR	Securities Markets Regulation
SSCC	Shenzhen Securities Communication Co. Ltd.
SSS	Securities Settlement System
STP	straight-through-processing
SWIFT	Society for Worldwide Interbank Financial Telecommunication
T2S	TARGET2-Securities
UCITS	Undertaking for Collective Investment in Transferable Securities
UITF	unit trust management company
USD	United States dollar
UTMC	unit trust management company

EXECUTIVE SUMMARY

The purpose of this study is to investigate the feasibility of applying the central securities depository and real-time gross settlement (CSD-RTGS) linkage model, which was originally proposed as a settlement engine for the Asian Bond Markets Initiative, to the delivery versus payment (DVP) settlement for the Asian passport collective investment scheme (CIS).

CIS passporting schemes are designed to facilitate the process of distributing CIS registered in the home economy into the host economy. Asian Bond Markets Initiative and CIS passporting schemes pursue the same goal of preventing the recurrence of the currency–maturity double mismatch.

This study starts with developments under the European CIS passport, known as UCITS, in order to review best practices in the implementation and harmonization of passport CIS DVP settlement.

In 2006, the European Commission published a white paper, *Enhancing the Single Market Framework for Investment Funds,* in which the European Commission suggested the standardization of the order routing process and the implementation of pan-European DVP settlement under the premise that post-trade standardization and a regional settlement engine are prerequisites for streamlining the operational efficiencies of CIS passport schemes.

In pursuit of post-trade harmonization, the European Fund and Asset Management Association established the Fund Processing Standardization Group in 2003, whereas the European Central Bank worked in tandem with regional CSDs and central banks to launch a pan-European settlement engine, TARGET2-Securities, in 2015.

This study found that a large number of ASEAN+3 members have in place a central processing platform for the standardization of CIS orders and that CIS in Asia can be passported under a bilateral framework such as the mutual recognition of funds or multilateral frameworks (e.g., Asia Region Funds Passport and ASEAN CIS).

However, the stakeholders of the Asian CIS industry and passport scheme seem to pay little attention to the significance of order routing harmonization and a viable DVP settlement environment.

This study also maintains that the CSD-RTGS linkage model proposed by CSIF has ample potential to be applied as a settlement engine for the cross-border transactions of other financial instruments, not just bonds. It is possible to achieve the post-trade standardization of CIS passporting and implementation of DVP settlement if the central platforms and DVP infrastructures are interlinked under the CSD-RTGS model.

Based on such considerations, this study recommends that CSIF should

- ▶ apply the CSD-RTGS DVP linkage not just to bonds, but also to CIS, as a pan-Asian settlement engine;
- ▶ form and lead a well-rounded post-trade consultative body designed to realize the broader application of the CSD-RTGS linkage model;
- ▶ advance research on ensuring the finality of the CSD-RTGS linkage model; and
- ▶ explore measures to bolster the efficiency of the CSD-RTGS linkage model if applied to both intra-regional bond and CIS transactions as an integrated DVP model.

The CIS market intelligence, assessments of ASEAN+3 infrastructure, and relevant terms and definitions are attached to this report as appendix and glossary.

INTRODUCTION

A. Background and Purpose of Research

For many decades, capital market integration in Asia progressed slower than in Europe due to the stark differences in economic size; degree of market development; and policies, laws, and regulations. However, Asian economies are becoming less and less fragmented and are striving for more cross-border interactions on the back of the advancement of information and communication technologies and the liberalization of capital flows, which has sped the pace of regional market integration.

Yet, the Achilles' heel of Asian financial markets has always been their vulnerability to a "double mismatch" between currency and maturity. To mitigate such a chronic problem, regional authorities have pushed for two ambitious attempts to channel Asian savings into regional investments through the Asian Bond Markets Initiative (ABMI) and the collective investment scheme (CIS) passport.[1]

ABMI is the practical response to what Asian economies grappled with in the aftermath of the 1997/98 Asian financial crisis. ABMI was first proposed by the delegation from the Republic of Korea at an informal meeting of Association of Southeast Asian Nations plus the People's Republic of China, Japan, and the Republic of Korea (ASEAN+3) deputy finance ministers in November 2002 and was largely supported by all 13 members.[2] On 7 August 2003, ABMI was officially launched at the ASEAN+3 Finance Ministers Meeting in Manila, with an aim to develop liquid and efficient bond markets in Asia so that savings in the region can be better utilized for regional investment.

The CIS passport schemes in Asia include multilateral frameworks, such as the Asia Region Funds Passport (ARFP)[3] through Asia-Pacific Economic Cooperation, and the Association of Southeast Asian Nations (ASEAN) CIS and bilateral frameworks, such as the PRC–Hong Kong Mutual Recognition of Funds (MRF).

ARFP and ASEAN CIS have set common rules on the registration and distribution of open-end public CIS to ensure effective cross-border transactions between home and host economies. The two passport schemes aim to facilitate the integration of Asian CIS markets via improved market access and regulatory harmonization under the mission of strengthening the capacity, expertise, and international

---

[1] A CIS passport refers to a multilateral framework in which a fund duly established in a home economy can be distributed in a host economy without an additional registration process.

[2] ASEAN+3 comprises the 10 members of ASEAN plus the People's Republic of China, Japan, and the Republic of Korea.

[3] ARFP participants include Australia, Japan, the Republic of Korea, New Zealand, and Thailand. ASEAN CIS participants include Malaysia, the Philippines, Singapore, and Thailand.

competitiveness of financial markets and the asset management industry in the region. Meanwhile, MRFs are promoted by participants who seek borderless transaction opportunities.

In May 2019, ABMI published the *ASEAN+3 Asian Bond Markets Initiative Medium-Term Road Map, 2019–2022* and defined its future direction as follows:

(i)   ABMI continues to support the development of local currency (LCY) bond markets in the region.

(ii)   ABMI will deepen its commitment and support to financial infrastructure.

(iii) ABMI will expand its scope of discussion to include other market activities closely linked with capital and bond market development in the ASEAN+3 region.

ASEAN+3 will strengthen collaboration to support regional financial cooperation initiatives. Written as part of the *ASEAN+3 Asian Bond Markets Initiative Medium-Term Road Map, 2019–2022*, this report sheds light on the cross-border transactions of passport CIS and explores the feasibility of applying the central securities depository and real-time gross settlement (CSD–RTGS) delivery versus payment (DVP) settlement model (CSD–RTGS linkage model) to such transactions. This research will contribute to building ideal regional market infrastructure as envisioned by the Cross-Border Settlement Infrastructure Forum (CSIF), which is committed to channeling Asian savings to regional investments, stimulating the development of regional financial institutions, and bolstering regional financial cooperation.

B.   Method and Scope of Research

The ultimate goal of this report is to study the feasibility of the CSD–RTGS linkage model, which was proposed by the CSIF of ABMI as a standardized clearing and settlement system for Asian bond markets, to see if it is possible to expand its application to the regional CIS industry and to recommend best practices accordingly.

For this, the research first takes readers to Europe to explore the Undertaking for Collective Investment in Transferable Securities (UCITS) and draw out key takeaways applicable to ASEAN+3. In particular, the report focuses on the background for adopting DVP for CIS settlement and the current DVP scheme for the European Central Bank settlement platform, TARGET2-Securities (T2S).

Then, the research focus shifts toward the Asian CIS industry. The CSIF consultant has studied the publications of regional CSDs and regulators, and conducted surveys to investigate the size of the CIS market, the existence of infrastructure for CIS subscription and redemption, DVP settlement in the course of CIS distribution, and the possibility of cross-border transaction.

In addition, the report provides current snapshots of Asian passport schemes and MRFs, the adoption of DVP, and pertinent laws and regulations.

Therefore, this research does not intend to test the theoretical validity (e.g., the purpose, background, or the characteristics of existing CIS passport schemes) or to analyze some desired effects (e.g., economic impact).

The contents of this report are much referenced from the prior literature of major economies and research institutions (e.g., periodicals and special reports, Q&A documents, and business handbooks), while the CIS market intelligence and statistics for ASEAN+3 are provided by regional members who have responded to a survey. Given the nature of the topic, which is the feasibility of the CSD-RTGS linkage model, the focal point of this report is post-trade processes.

II

CHARACTERISTICS OF COLLECTIVE INVESTMENT SCHEMES

A.   Basic Information on Collective Investment Scheme Products

Collective investment scheme (CIS) products belong to the domain of asset management, which is defined as a financial service to manage investments on behalf of clients in exchange for fees or commissions. What investors mostly expect from asset managers are cost-effectiveness, diversification, and professional investing. Due to the inevitable informational asymmetry between investors and asset managers, CIS products should be designed to ensure investor protection through more complex safeguards and operational processes (e.g., strict compliance checks by custodians, net asset value (NAV) calculation by an independent administrator) than when directly investing in stocks or bonds.[4]

CIS can be categorized as publicly offered CIS (public CIS) or privately placed CIS (private CIS), depending on the degree of regulations such as the number of investors and permitted assets.

Public CIS are offered to the general public via securities firms, banks, or other distribution channels.[5] Public CIS are strongly regulated in terms of investor protection since they are offered to retail investors who tend to lack professional investing skills and experience. Such regulations include stringent requirements on asset management, external audits, prospectus requirements, and concentration limits. As for the portfolio of public CIS, the concentration of assets in a single product or shares issued by an identical entity cannot exceed a certain threshold (e.g., 10% and 20%, respectively, in the Republic of Korea).[6]

Public CIS may come in many different forms depending on investment strategies (e.g., equity CIS, bond CIS, or mixed CIS) and terms (e.g., short-, mid-, and long-term CIS). Simply put, any CIS falls into the category of public CIS except for hedge funds and private equity funds, which are two major components of private CIS.[7]

Private CIS are privately offered to investors who are high-net-worth investors (including institutional investors) and fewer in number than the minimum threshold for public CIS. Either in the form of a hedge fund or a private equity fund, a private CIS is established by a contract among individuals. Since

---

4   For example, the relevant laws and regulations in the Republic of Korea mandate that trustees, who are typically custodians, monitor the activities of asset management companies.

5   As for public CIS, the requirement on the number of investors may differ depending on jurisdictions, e.g., ≥25 (Thailand), ≥50 (Republic of Korea, and Japan), and ≥100 (Indonesia).

6   It is prescribed in the pertinent law of the Republic of Korea on public CIS.

7   It is the common way to categorize private CIS in the Republic of Korea.

asset managers are given much more discretion for managing assets, private CIS can not only deliver more profits but also are exposed to more risks than public CIS.

Also, CIS may be established in the following forms:

(i)   Umbrella CIS give investors the option of switching from one subsidiary CIS to another (e.g., from an equity CIS to a bond CIS) within the same structure. Thus, umbrella CIS investors can respond to market changes.

(ii)   Master-feeder CIS is a two-tier structure where the feeder CIS collects capital from investors and channels it to the master CIS, while both the master and feeder CIS are managed by the same asset manager. A master-feeder CIS is often favored by managers as a way to streamline asset management.

(iii) An exchange-traded fund (ETF) tracks an index, a sector, a commodity, or other assets (e.g., crude oil, gold, KOSPI200, or NIKKEI 225). ETFs can be bought and sold on a regulated exchange in the same way as regular stocks.

B.   Settlement Process for a Collective Investment Scheme

1.   Subscription

Subscription refers to the process of collecting capital from investors in exchange for the designated number of units or shares, thus, securing the financial source for collective investing.

Asset managers can execute their portfolio strategies once their CIS are offered as disclosed in a prospectus and investor capital is duly collected via subscription. Many economies around the world allow asset management companies to delegate a distributor that is equipped with a broad distribution network to offer CIS on their behalf, although it is still possible to vertically integrate management and distribution under a single governance structure.[8]

It is important to note when exactly ownership is determined during the subscription process. Retail investors may believe that their ownership is confirmed (and their units are issued) once their money is wired to their distributor. However, it is not the distributor that issues the units. In fact, the units are actually issued when the money arrives at the custodian or fund administrator designated by the asset management company—the exact timing for settlement finality based on payment of cash and delivery of units.

2.   Redemption

How the owner retrieves money invested in CIS, or how the owner redeems units, may differ depending on the legal structure of CIS. As for open-end CIS, the owner can make a redemption order at any time at the place of subscription (e.g., distributor) and wait until the units are redeemed at the NAV calculated by the asset management company (or CIS administrator). However, closed-end CIS can be

---

[8]   CIS are mostly offered by securities firms, banks, and insurance companies, while there are also online distribution channels such as a fund supermarket.

redeemed only if listed on a regulated market. Settlement-wise, the redemption process is finalized via payment of cash and deletion of the redeemed units.

3. *Exercise of Unit Holder Rights*

Once units are acquired through subscription, investor details such as names or addresses are recorded in a register, based on which unit holders can claim their ownership against asset management companies (e.g., participation in unitholder meetings, exercise of voting rights, and rights to receive dividends).

C. Various Market Players for Collective Investment Schemes

Unlike direct investing, CIS are not directly managed by investors. The authority of investors for asset management is delegated to experts who formulate and execute investment strategies, keep custody of assets, and process settlement and other post-trade operations. Such delegated work is performed by asset management companies either though in-house vertical integration or outsourcing contracts.

Once a suitable CIS is chosen and subscribed to, investors authorize an asset manager to make professional investment decisions on the pooled capital based on their diversification strategies.

Asset managers pursue professional division of work through in-house vertical integration or collaboration with their contracted partners. When offering their CIS products, asset managers in many parts of the world rely on independent distributors that have a powerful distribution network (e.g., securities firms, banks, and insurance companies). In general, the investment cash and units are safely kept by the custodian designated by the asset manager. Plus, NAV is objectively and accurately calculated either by a third-party administrator (or directly by the asset management company at times).

The diverse roles divided by function are not performed in silos but through a close-knit communication network. Once investors place a subscription order at the distributor, the corresponding cash should be transferred to the custodian designated by the asset management company, while the transaction details should go to the administrator for accurate NAV calculation. Be it in-house vertical integration or outsourcing structure, a chain of cooperative network ensures the smooth workflow—from distribution to management, custody, and (finally) NAV calculation.

Another aspect of CIS investing is the emphasis on investor protection. If not highly sophisticated, investors are not able to oversee all of the activities of the asset manager and determine if the CIS is thoroughly managed in accordance with the prospectus. However, the assets of the clients are nominally managed by the asset manager for the purpose of professional investing, while the entire management of activities are subject to the strict oversight of custodians to ensure the best interest of end-investors.

The post-trade side of CIS investing mentioned above can be streamlined by a central straight-through-processing (STP) platform (e.g., FundNet of Korea Securities Depository [KSD], Central Moneymarket Unit [CMU] Fund Order Routing and Settlement Service [FORS] of the Hong Kong

Monetary Authority [HKMA], S-INVEST of PT Kustodian Sentral Efek Indonesia [KSEI] or the Indonesia Central Securities Depository, and FundConnext of the Digital Access Platform Company Limited [DAP]). Such infrastructure is valuable because CIS markets can become less costly and more efficient by shifting away from fragmentation and achieving economies of scale during the course of post-trade integration.

D. Collective Investment Scheme Passporting as a Driver for Cross-Border Transactions

A cross-border transaction is defined here as buying or selling units of a CIS domiciled in their home economy by host economy investors. The transaction may come in two directions: (i) inbound transaction (foreign-domiciled CIS sold at home), and (ii) outbound transaction (home-domiciled CIS sold abroad).

The 2016 research of the Korea Capital Market Institute implies that several factors are at play behind the cross-border offering of CIS: track records, fees and commissions, regulations, and post-trade infrastructure.[9] Track records matter most when selecting a CIS. As for a public CIS, in particular, a track record is often received as a key indicator for expected returns since it is hard for investors to find any other indicative references.

The second factor that comes into play is fees and commissions. It is found that investors are more attracted to CIS that incur lower fees and commissions.[10]

Another factor is administrative hurdles that stem from national differences in laws and regulations. A CIS cannot cross the border if some of its establishment requirements are deemed unacceptable in the host economy.

With this in mind, Europe has long integrated its regional CIS markets under its internationally recognized passport brand, UCITS, harmonizing regulatory hurdles, demonstrating time-tested track records, lowering fees and commissions, and streamlining relevant mid-and-back office operations and infrastructure. In recent years, Asia seems to be following suit with its own passport brands (including ARFP, ASEAN CIS, and MRF) in order to increase cross-border transactions in Asia and beyond.

---

[9] Korea Capital Market Institute (KCMI). 2016. Globalization of the Korean Asset Management Industry: Future Directions and Challenges. *KCMI Research Series 16-01*. Seoul.

[10] This conclusion is based on the comparative analysis of fees and commissions related to 46,580 public CIS broadly distributed in 18 countries in 2002 with particular focus on the following insights:
- The larger the transaction volume, the lower the fees and commissions.
- The broader the distribution market footprint (especially including high-tax countries), the higher the fees and commissions.
- Fees and commissions are lower if the fund is offered to institutional investors.
- The stronger the safeguards for investors, the lower the fees and commissions.

III

EUROPE'S PASSPORT BRAND: UNDERTAKING FOR COLLECTIVE INVESTMENT IN TRANSFERABLE SECURITIES

A. The Inception of Undertaking for Collective Investment in Transferable Securities

In 1985, as indirect investing was gaining ground in Europe, the European Commission established the Undertaking for Collective Investment in Transferable Securities (UCITS)—a common regulatory framework on collective investment schemes investing in transferable securities—with a mission to turn Europe into a single integrated market.

UCITS governs the registration and licensing for open-end CIS, the asset managers of such collective investment scheme (CIS), permitted assets, operations, the roles and responsibilities of asset managers and depositaries, supervision, and information disclosure.[11] UCITS was designed to streamline the European asset management industry by achieving economies of scale and ultimately creating one integrated market for CIS in Europe.

The net assets of UCITS and Alternative Investment Funds (AIFs) recorded an increase of 4.5% in the first quarter of 2021, reaching EUR19.6 trillion (Figure 1). UCITS net assets increased by 5.6% during the same period.[12] The solid growth of UCITS was driven by robust stock market gains and strong net sales. UCITS and AIFs attracted EUR201 billion of net inflows in the first quarter of 2021. Net sales of UCITS amounted to EUR169 billion, compared to EUR226 billion in the fourth quarter of 2020.[13]

The NAV of UCITS CIS increased from EUR4.3 trillion in 2008 to EUR10.0 trillion in 2019 (Figure 2).

Many UCITS CIS are sold in economies with large and mid-sized CIS markets. As a highly trusted brand for cross-border transactions, UCITS CIS are broadly marketed in Europe and many other regions including Asia, North America, and Africa. According to the PricewaterhouseCoopers' (PwC) 2021 edition of the *Global Fund Distribution Poster*, UCITS CIS sold outside of the European Union (EU) are mostly sold in Asia (Figure 3).

The share of Asia in global CIS distribution has been on the rise since 2016, according to PwC.

In Asia, UCITS CIS are mostly sold in Singapore. This is followed by Hong Kong, China and the Republic of Korea (Table 1).

---

[11]   A depositary, as defined under EU law, is an entity eligible to act in a safekeeping and fiduciary capacity in the EU member state of a collective investment scheme (fund), as well as providing global custody services. But a depository generally refers to a CSD.

[12]   The CISs domiciled in Europe are largely divided into UCITS and AIFs.

[13]   EFAMA. 2021. *Trends in the European Investment Fund Industry in the First Quarter of 2021.*

Figure 1: The European Collective Investment Scheme Market at a Glance

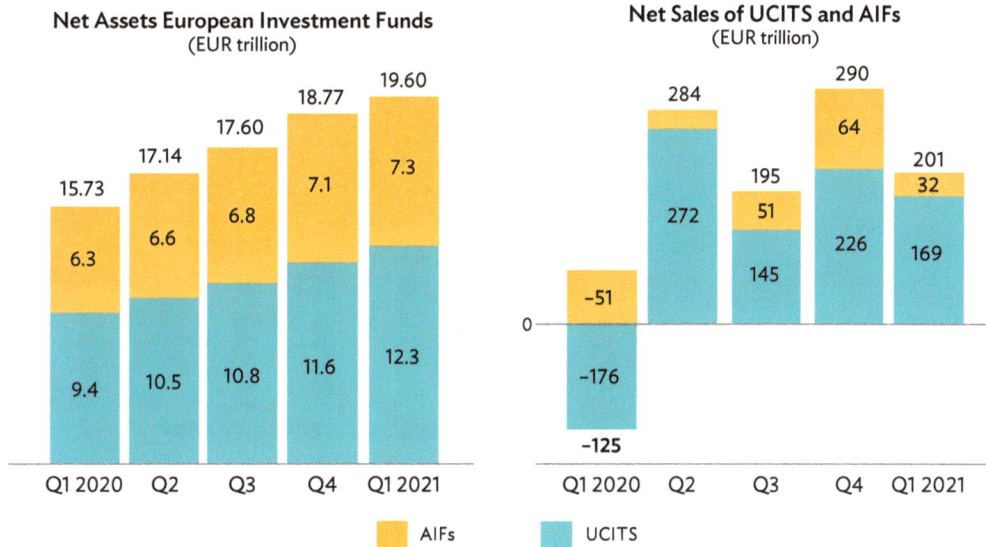

Net Assets European Investment Funds
(EUR trillion)

Quarter	UCITS	AIFs	Total
Q1 2020	9.4	6.3	15.73
Q2	10.5	6.6	17.14
Q3	10.8	6.8	17.60
Q4	11.6	7.1	18.77
Q1 2021	12.3	7.3	19.60

Net Sales of UCITS and AIFs
(EUR trillion)

Quarter	UCITS	AIFs	Total
Q1 2020	−176	−51	−125
Q2	272	284	
Q3	145	51	195
Q4	226	64	290
Q1 2021	169	32	201

AIFs ■ UCITS ■

AIF = Alternative Investment Fund, EUR = euro, Q = quarter, UCITS = Undertaking for Collective Investment in Transferable Securities.

Source: European Fund and Asset Management Association. 2021. *Trends in the European Investment Fund Industry in the First Quarter of 2021.*

Figure 2: Net Assets of Undertakings for Collective Investment in Transferable Securities in the European Union
(EUR trillion)

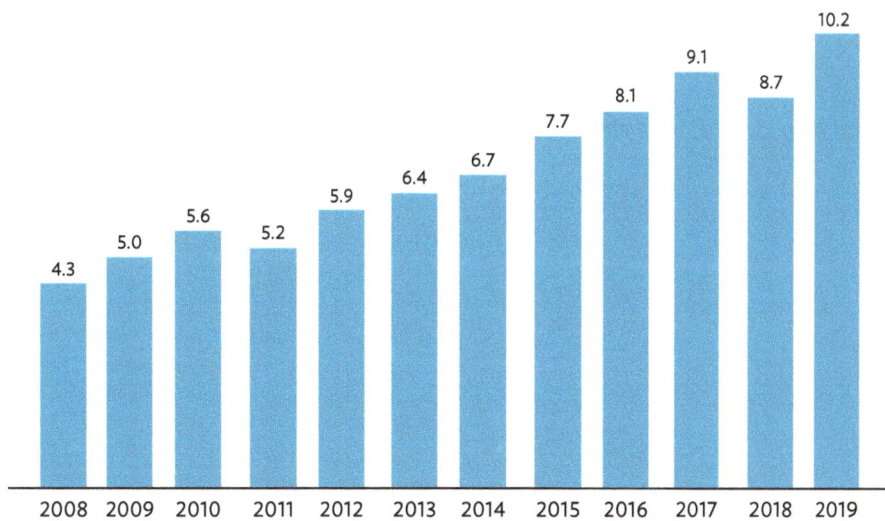

Year	Value
2008	4.3
2009	5.0
2010	5.6
2011	5.2
2012	5.9
2013	6.4
2014	6.7
2015	7.7
2016	8.1
2017	9.1
2018	8.7
2019	10.2

EUR = euro, UCITS = Undertaking for Collective Investment in Transferable Securities.

Note: Data include UCITS domiciled in the United Kingdom and the Netherlands (representing 13% of net assets at year-end 2019). Data also include exchange-traded funds and UCITS that invest primarily in other funds.

Source: European Fund and Asset Management Association. 2020. *ICI Research Perspective.* October. Brussels.

Figure 3: Global Collective Investment Scheme Distribution Trend by Year

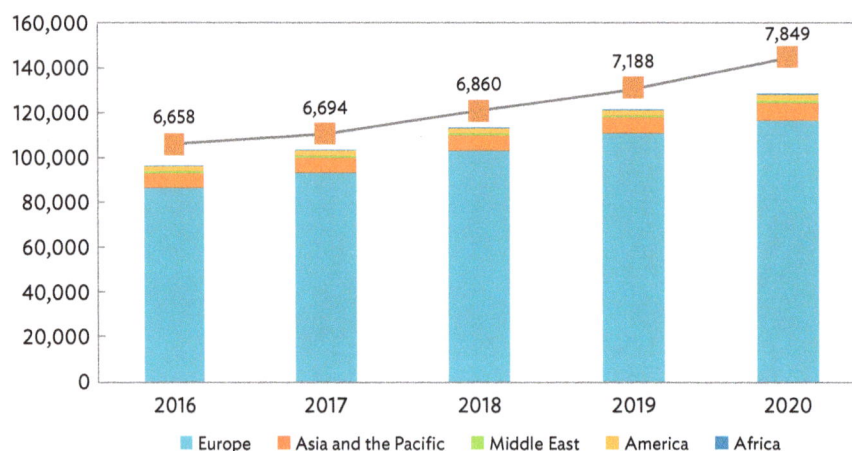

Note: The unit of reference in this figure is the number of collective investment schemes sold.

Source: Cross-Border Settlement Infrastructure Forum (CSIF) based on PwC. 2021. *Global Fund Distribution Poster*. Luxembourg.

Table 1: Global Collective Investment Scheme Distribution

Distribution Market	Fund Domiciles							
	Luxembourg	Ireland	France	Jersey	UK	Germany	Others	Total
Europe	65,289	39,502	3,846	3,115	1,410	860	2,520	116,542
Asia and the Pacific	5,331	2,004	47	31	90	31	315	7,849
Middle East	693	319	2	9	10		39	1,072
America	1,160	787	99	1	80	43	566	2,736
Africa	178	110		12	13		9	322
Total	**72,651**	**42,722**	**3,994**	**3,168**	**1,603**	**934**	**3,449**	**128,521**

Asia and the Pacific	Fund Domiciles							
	Luxembourg	Ireland	France	Jersey	UK	Germany	Others	Total
Singapore	2,436	1,409	38	9	63	17	196	4,168
Hong Kong, China	908	169			10	1	14	1,102
Republic of Korea	499	92			6		2	599
Japan	79	53	5	21		4	6	168
Brunei Darussalam	95							95
Australia	28	35	1	1	1		23	89
New Zealand	2	1					5	8
Viet Nam	3							3
People's Republic of China							3	3
Others	1,281	245	3		10	8	66	1,613
Total	**5,331**	**2,004**	**47**	**31**	**90**	**30**	**315**	**7,848**

UK = United Kingdom.

Note: All data are as of the end of 2020.

Source: Cross-Border Settlement Infrastructure Forum (CSIF) based on PwC. 2021. *Global Fund Distribution Poster*. Luxembourg.

B.   Overview and Past Journey of Undertaking for Collective Investment in Transferable Securities

As of 2020, the UCITS available for download from the European Securities and Market Association (ESMA) comprises 14 chapters, 119 articles, and 4 annexes.[14]

Chapter II describes the purpose, scope, and definition of UCITS. The key points of the chapter include the following:

- UCITS should be transposed into the legal territories of EU member states.
- UCITS CIS are collective investment schemes that can be established in the form of a common CIS under contract law, an investment trust, or an investment company.
- UCITS CIS must be open-end CIS offered and sold to the public.[15]
- The meaning of essential terms including "UCITS Home Member State" and "UCITS Host Member State" is clearly defined.

The major parts of the remaining contents are as follows:

- Chapter II (Authorization of UCITS) deals with how a UCITS CIS is authorized in a Home Member State.[16]
- Chapter III (Obligations Regarding Management Companies) describes the eligibility and requirements of asset management companies (including initial capital threshold).
- Chapter IV (Obligations Regarding the Depositary) explains how depositaries are regulated to ensure that the sale, issue, repurchase, redemption, and cancellation of units of the UCITS are carried out in accordance with the applicable national law and the CIS rules or instruments of incorporation.[17]
- Chapter V (Obligations Regarding Investment Companies) clarifies what information must be provided by asset management companies and distributors for investor protection.
- Chapter XI contains special provisions applicable to UCITS that market their units in member states other than those in which they are established.

Since its inception in 1975, what can be referred to as UCITS I has evolved into UCITS V. There are ongoing discussions about the transition to UCITS VI.

The first UCITS European directive set out a common set of rules for the cross-border distribution of CIS, namely the "European passport," and was designed with the retail consumer in mind, enshrining appropriate levels of protection for these investors.

---

[14]   European Parliament. 2009. Directive 2009/65/EC of the European Parliament and of the Council of Coordination of Laws, Regulations and Administrative Provisions relating to Undertakings for Collective Investment in Transferable Securities (UCITS).

[15]   UCITS Article 3(a), (b).

[16]   CIS in Europe comprise those regulated under UCITS and the ones exempt from UCITS. The latter includes AIFs.

[17]   UCITS Article 22 3(a).

While the new regime did prove successful, flaws soon became apparent and early in the 1990s, the EU Council of Ministers failed to agree on measures to reform the regime and abandoned plans for a UCITS II.

Two new directives, the Product Directive and the Management Directive, collectively known as UCITS III, introduced new rules that were implemented in Ireland in 2003. The rules related to the operations of management companies, prospectuses, consumer choice, and investor protection. Most significantly, they broadened the asset classes UCITS were permitted to invest in. These permitted asset classes were further clarified in the Eligible Assets Directive, which took effect in 2007.

In 2009, a new wave of amendments known as UCITS IV were approved, providing, among other things, for the management company (ManCo) passport, a revised notification procedure for cross-border CIS sales, the introduction of a Key Investor Information Document, the creation of master feeder structures, and enhanced regulatory cooperation. These rules were introduced in Ireland in 2011.

In 2014, the UCITS V directive was adopted by the European Commission, focusing on harmonizing the role and the liability of depositaries, remuneration policies for UCITS managers, and sanctions for breaches of UCITS legislation. UCITS V took effect in early 2016.

C.   The Rise of Undertaking for Collective Investment in Transferable Securities as an Iconic Passport Brand

The success of UCITS lies in the rise of Luxembourg as a CIS center where the first UCITS CIS was established on 30 March 1988 and where the largest UCITS domiciliation in the world currently takes place.[18] This section of the report sheds light on when and how Luxembourg has put itself on the map as a central domicile for UCITS CIS.

In the 1990s, the physical location of Luxembourg mattered greatly at a time when internet-driven connectivity was still a faraway idea and geographical proximity was most important. With Belgium, France, and Germany on its doorstep, Luxembourg was located near many big fund houses in Europe.

During the 1990s, a large number of fund houses chose Luxembourg to avoid the higher withholding taxes (e.g., 30% in Germany and 35% in Switzerland) in their jurisdictions. For instance, as the asset transfer from German and Swiss domestic CIS to Luxembourg was accelerated throughout 1992, the importance of these two countries' fund promoters was such that they managed just under 50% of all Luxembourg-domiciled CIS in September 1992.[19]

---

[18]   Thomson Reuters. 2019. *Symbiosis in the Evolution of UCITS, 1988–2018: Three Decades of Funds Industry Transformation.*

[19]   The term "fund promoter" (also known as "fund sponsor" or "fund initiator") is a frequently used industry jargon referring to asset managers that set up a CIS and determine its terms and conditions.

With interest rates increasingly plunging, bond investors gravitated toward bond CIS, while the United States (US) investment capital for dot-com enterprises was quickly collected by equity CIS. The initial move to bond CIS occurred in 1993, as the industry in Luxembourg grew by USD83.5 billion, with 67% of this growth (USD56 billion) coming from new CIS launches (343 new CIS in total). The bulk (83%) of this new money went into bond CIS.

Meanwhile, equity assets nearly doubled in 1993 and increased their share of the Luxembourg CIS industry by more than 10%. Exemplifying this boom, the CIS investing in technology and telecom stocks attracted USD16.0 billion by the end of 1999, up from a mere USD2.6 billion a year earlier. Over 40% of these assets came from CIS launched in 1999 alone.

D.   Post-Trade Reform of Undertaking for Collective Investment in Transferable Securities: Messaging, Order Routing, and Settlement

In 2006, the European Commission was authorized by the European Council and the European Parliament to draft and publish the white paper on *Enhancing the Single Market Framework for Investment Funds*.[20] The paper was initiated out of concern that the European asset management markets were largely fragmented when compared to the US and that Europe might not be able to close the gap under the 2006 version of UCITS.

The paper pointed out the weaknesses of the UCITS framework and suggested viable solutions to transform Europe into a single integrated market where investors can be better protected in a low-cost, highly efficient transaction environment. The suggested solutions dealt with two major issues: transaction inefficiencies and investor protection.

As demonstrated in Table 2, the issues raised by the white paper have been duly addressed over time as UCITS advances toward better versions (e.g., UCITS IV and UCITS V). The paper mentioned how to streamline and standardize the settlement and other post-trade processing for CIS without compromising the regulatory architecture of UCITS.

In the early 2000s, UCITS was criticized for lagging behind the front-end developments of the CIS industry, especially due to the inefficiencies of post-trade processing. The later sections of this chapter describe the European quest for post-trade standardization under UCITS through the particular prism of messaging, order processing, and settlement.

---

[20] Commission of the European Communities. 2006. *White Paper on Enhancing the Single Market Framework for Investment Funds*. Brussels.

Box 1: Highlights of the White Paper on Enhancing the Single Market Framework for Investment Funds

Transaction Inefficiencies

▶ **Facilitation of Cross-Border CIS Mergers**

The Undertaking for Collective Investment in Transferable Securities (UCITS) market was populated by collective investment scheme (CIS) of suboptimal size; some 54% of UCITS CIS had less than EUR50 million in assets under management. Consequently, important economies of scale remained unexploited and the end-investor bore unnecessarily high costs. Research estimated that costs could be annually reduced by between EUR5 billion and EUR6 billion. The CIS merger was permitted by UCITS IV in 2011.

▶ **Asset Pooling**

Asset pooling allows simultaneous management of assets gathered by different CIS while maintaining a local CIS presence in different target markets. The skills and costs of successful management teams can be spread over a wider pool of assets. These techniques are not only relevant for CIS but also as a possible model for pension CIS. Pooling was increasingly used in some European economies. However, there were significant barriers to cross-border asset pooling.

▶ **Management Company Passport**[a]

In 2006, CIS management groups needed to establish a fully functional management company in each economy where they domiciled a CIS. The local substance requirements in each economy pushed up costs and prevented scale and specialization gains.

▶ **Efficiency Improvements Requiring No Changes to UCITS**

- Strict deadline for authorization in country of domicile.[b]

- Message routing and CIS order processing and settlement: Order processing did not keep pace with the growth of the CIS market and changes in distribution systems. It was characterized by higher operational risks, longer processing delays and, inevitably, higher costs.[c]

- Depositary passport: The freedom to appoint a depositary in another European economy did not seem to hold out the prospect of significant gains. Depositary functions accounted for a low proportion of total CIS costs and were largely exhausted through extensive use of delegation. Any marginal benefits seemed to be considerably outweighed by the scale of adjustments that would need to be undertaken to UCITS to harmonize the responsibilities and functions of the depositary.[d]

Investor Protection

▶ **Simplified Prospectus**[e]

The simplified prospectus was intended to provide investors and intermediaries with basic information about the possible risks, associated charges, and expected outcomes of the respective product. However, it manifestly failed. In most cases, the document was too long and not understood by its intended readers.

▶ **Distribution Systems Putting Investor Interests First**

Distribution systems that match investor demand with CIS supply must work efficiently. They must deliver products that meet the needs of individual investors on competitive terms. In 2007, CIS distribution accounted for the biggest single component of costs in the CIS industry, ranging from 46% of total costs in France to 75% in Italy.

The Markets in Financial Instruments Directive provides the tools to manage these concerns. Its implementing measures stipulate that inducements must be disclosed and can only be provided where they are in the interests of the client.

The issues and solutions described in the white paper were mostly reflected in UCITS IV and UCITS V, thus, paving the way for Europe's progress with regional market integration characterized as accelerated cross-border transaction of UCITS CIS, reduced transaction costs, solid investor protection, and transparent CIS management.

[a] A management company passport was permitted by UCITS IV in 2011.
[b] In 2006, the approval for the offering of a host economy CIS took as long as 6 weeks, which has since been uniformly reduced to 10 business days. Further details can be found in Section 1.5.2.1 Authorization of UCITS CIS.
[c] This problem is increasingly mitigated by inter-central securities depository linkage of CIS platforms and TARGET2-Securities, messaging standardization, and straight-through-processing (STP)-based operational enhancement. Further details can be found in Section 1.5 UCITS and TARGET2-Securities.
[d] There are ongoing debates on this matter that will be further elucidated by the upcoming UCITS VI.
[e] As a complementary solution, UCITS IV mandates that a three-page key investor information document should be provided to investors.

Source: Commission of the European Communities. 2006. *White Paper on Enhancing the Single Market Framework for Investment Funds*. Brussels.

Table 2: Developments of Undertaking for Collective Investment in Transferable Securities

UCITS I (1985)	UCITS II Abandoned	UCITS III (2001)	UCITS IV (2009)	UCITS V (2016)	UCITS VI (To be determined)
Original UCITS directive published.	UCITS II was abandoned in 1998 after EU member states failed to reach an agreement on its scope and purpose. Key provisions included much of the framework of UCITS III.	Firms were given until February 2007 to ensure their funds were UCITS III compliant. UCITS III was divided into two distinctive directives: **Management directive:** Creation of the European Passport whereby a UCITS fund authorized in its home state could be sold anywhere within the EU. Also required the use of a simplified prospectus detailing the key features of a fund. **Product directive:** Allowed for investments in a wider range of asset classes with a corresponding distinction between non-sophisticated and sophisticated funds.	UCITS IV was effective on 1 July 2011. Key provisions included the following: - Streamlined regulator-to-regulator notification procedures - Management company passport created - Key Investor Information (KII) document replaced the simplified prospectus - Master-feeder fund structures are introduced - Framework for domestic and cross-border fund mergers is created	UCITS V amendments were proposed by the EU Commission in July 2012 and approved by the European Parliament in April 2014. - Depositary regime updates, including their appointment and eligible entities, oversight duties, cash-monitoring duties, safe-keeping duties, delegation, and overall liability - Establishment of remuneration policies and practices that promote sound and effective risk management and do not encourage risk-taking. Remuneration structures will need to include rules on variable and fixed compensation, including a requirement that at least 50% of variable remuneration be in the form of units - Creation of a sanctions regime and whistle-blowing procedures for reporting incidents to authorities	Potential areas covered include the following: - Eligible assets, use of derivatives and efficient portfolio management techniques - Liquidity management - Depositary passport - Money market funds - Long-term investment funds - Consistency with AIFM Directive

AIFM = Alternative Investment Fund Managers, EU = European Union, UCITS = Undertaking for Collective Investment in Transferable Securities.

Source: Cross-Border Settlement Infrastructure Forum (CSIF) based on Ernst & Young LLP. 2015. *European Mutual Funds: An Introduction to UCITS for US Asset Managers*. London.

E.   Europe Fund and Asset Management Association and the Pan-European Standardization of Collective Investment Scheme Settlement

In 2003, the European Fund and Asset Management Association (EFAMA) established the Fund Processing Standardization Group (FPSG) to draw up recommendations for the efficiency enhancement of post-trade processing for cross-border transaction of CIS. FPSG is made up of expert practitioners representing the European CIS industry (e.g., asset management companies, custodians, transfer agents, CIS processing hubs, and existing standard setting organizations).

The inefficiencies of CIS processing are still apparent in cross-border distribution. This is a very important segment of the European CIS industry. The efforts of FPSG to streamline the post-trade aspects of the European CIS industry are well described in the 2018 version of *Standardization of Funds Processing in Europe: Order and Settlement Transfers Holding and Transaction Reporting* (hereinafter "the FPSG report").

Revised five times since its initial publication in September 2008, the FPSG report recommends how to standardize order processing, settlement, fee structure, corporate actions, and notifications, and how to embrace fintech, distributed ledger technology, and other new innovative solutions.

The FPSG report starts with general recommendations for the European CIS industry and describes in the later sections the generic models and issues as well as specific suggestions for processing enhancement.[21] Among the contents in the 2018 version of the report, only the subscription-related part is quoted herein.

The general recommendations offered in the FPSG report are summarized in Box 2.

Figure 4 shows the generic processing model for order and settlement as described in the FPSG report.

As seen from the above, there are five discrete roles in the overall order and settlement process (Box 3)

The recommendations of the FPSG report also include order-and-settlement specific recommendations (Box 4).

Meanwhile, EFAMA works with the Society for Worldwide Interbank Financial Telecommunication (SWIFT) to monitor and analyze the developments of CIS processing standardization based on data from Luxembourg and Ireland, and publishes the results on an annual basis.

---

[21]   For details, see section 3 of the FPSG report.

Box 2: Highlights of Fund Processing Standardization Group Report

▶ **Straight-through-Processing Facilitation**

- More orders should be electronically processed rather than relying on manual operations.
- Asset management companies should arrange for standardized reference and Markets in Financial Instruments Directive II sales data (including target market and cost information) to be made available for their collective investment scheme (CIS) to facilitate their transaction.
- Where legal or regulatory barriers or constraints to the implementation of these recommendations exist, national associations should work with the relevant government or regulator to remove or alleviate them.
- International Organization for Standardization(ISO) Standard Identifier should be used.
- Where possible, financial institutions should be identified using their Legal Entity Identifier code or Bank Identifier Code.
- CIS providers should use International Securities Identification Number (ISIN) codes for all of their CIS products from the lowest level.
- Wherever possible, countries, currencies or all other items should be identified using the relevant ISO standards.

▶ **Messaging Standards**

- The communications between client-side and CIS-side institutions should, as far as possible, be electronic.
- ISO 20022 is recognized as the single European standard for CIS-related messaging going forward and should be the basis for electronic communications in this area.
- Messages should be used for the purposes for which they were designed and in accordance with any market practice that may be published by the Securities Market Practice Group or its constituent, the National Market Practice Group.
- Proprietary message standards between client-side and CIS-side institutions should be avoided.

Source: European Fund and Asset Management Association. 2018. *Standardization of Funds Processing in Europe.*

The total automation rate reached 93.2% in the fourth quarter (Q4) of 2020, compared to 91.8% in Q4 2019. This increase was accompanied with a decrease in the manual processing rate (from 8.2% in Q4 2019 to 6.8% in Q4 2020), mainly to the benefit of Proprietary File Transfer Protocol (Table 3).[22]

The use of the International Organization for Standardization (ISO) messaging standard decreased by 2.9 percentage points in the course of 2020 to reach 59.4% in Q4 2020 (against 62.3% in Q4 2019). Figure 5 shows the various rates of evolution since the beginning of 2018.

---

[22] European Fund and Asset Management Association. 2021. *Fund Processing Standardisation Annual Report on Automation and Standardisation of Cross-Border Funds Orders in 2020.*

Figure 4: Generic Processing Model for Order and Settlement

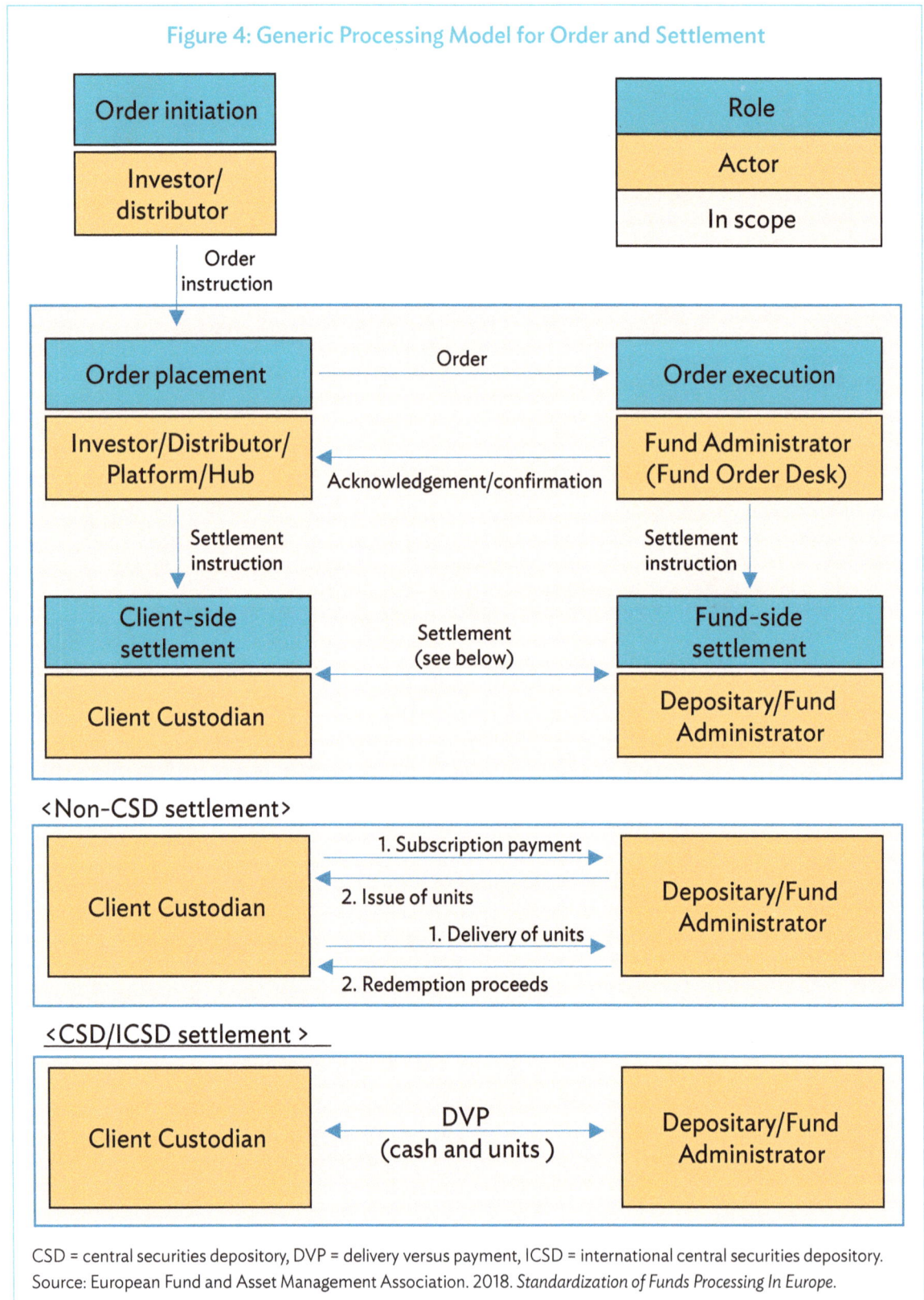

Order initiation
Investor/ distributor

Role
Actor
In scope

Order instruction

Order placement	Order →	Order execution
Investor/Distributor/ Platform/Hub	← Acknowledgement/confirmation	Fund Administrator (Fund Order Desk)

Settlement instruction

Settlement instruction

Client-side settlement	Settlement (see below)	Fund-side settlement
Client Custodian		Depositary/Fund Administrator

‹Non-CSD settlement›

Client Custodian	1. Subscription payment → ← 2. Issue of units 1. Delivery of units → ← 2. Redemption proceeds	Depositary/Fund Administrator

‹CSD/ICSD settlement ›

Client Custodian	← DVP (cash and units) →	Depositary/Fund Administrator

CSD = central securities depository, DVP = delivery versus payment, ICSD = international central securities depository.
Source: European Fund and Asset Management Association. 2018. *Standardization of Funds Processing In Europe.*

Box 3: Overall Order and Settlement Process of Fund Processing Standardization Group Report

▶ **Order initiation:** Initiation of the order by the end investor and communication through the placement stage, directly or through one or more intermediaries.

▶ **Order placement:** Communication of the order to the collective investment scheme (CIS)-side institution by the dealing function of the client-side institution and subsequent issue of the client-side settlement instructions.

▶ **Order execution:** Receipt, acceptance, and processing of the order by the CIS-side institution as agent for the CIS or (in the United Kingdom) as principal.

▶ **Client-side settlement:** Arranging for payment to be made for units purchased or for title to be given up to units sold.

Source: European Fund and Asset Management Association. 2018. *Standardization of Funds Processing in Europe.*

Box 4: Recommendations of the Fund Processing Standardization Group Report

▶ Where the transaction relates to an existing holding, the account (where relevant) should be identified by way of the collective investment scheme (CIS)-side institution's reference. Otherwise, a standard set of registration details should be provided. Where possible, a unique identifier for an investor should be used (e.g., CONCAT in the case of natural persons and subject to requirements of data protection laws and a Legal Entity Identifier [LEI] code in the case of legal entities in a broad sense).[a]

▶ Transfer agent systems and CIS registers should be able to accept and store account numbers or distributor references (where applicable) provided by client-side institutions to allow proper identification of the holding. Uniqueness may be ensured by reference to the Bank Identifier Code (BIC) or LEI code of the distributor associated with the account. In case of a one-to-one relationship between BIC and LEI, preference should be given to LEI. If the BIC contains a higher granularity than the LEI, then the LEI and the BIC1 should be sent. In the longer term, an International Bank Account Number-type approach (with codes being issued by the client-side institution) should be considered for the purposes of establishing a unique account holder reference.

▶ The industry should adopt a standard minimum set of account standing data to be provided in relation to a new or existing holding for which the client-side institution does not have the holder reference. Where possible, a unique identifier should be used for an investor (e.g., CONCAT in the case of natural persons and subject to requirements of data protection laws and LEI in the case of legal entities).

[a] CONCAT refers to a concatenation that consists of four elements: (i) two-character ISO country code (as for all personal identifiers), (ii) birth date (YYYY/MM/DD), (iii) first five characters of first name, and (iv) first five characters of surname.

Source: European Fund and Asset Management Association. 2018. *Standardization of Funds Processing in Europe.*

Table 3: Total Automation Rate Evolution, 2018–2020
(%)

Year	Q1	Q2	Q3	Q4
2018	88.4	89.4	89.5	90.4
2019	90.2	90.6	91.0	91.8
2020	91.7	91.9	92.6	93.2

Q = quarter.
Source: European Fund and Asset Management Association. 2021. *Fund Processing Standardisation Annual Report on Automation and Standardisation of Cross-Border Funds Orders in 2020.*

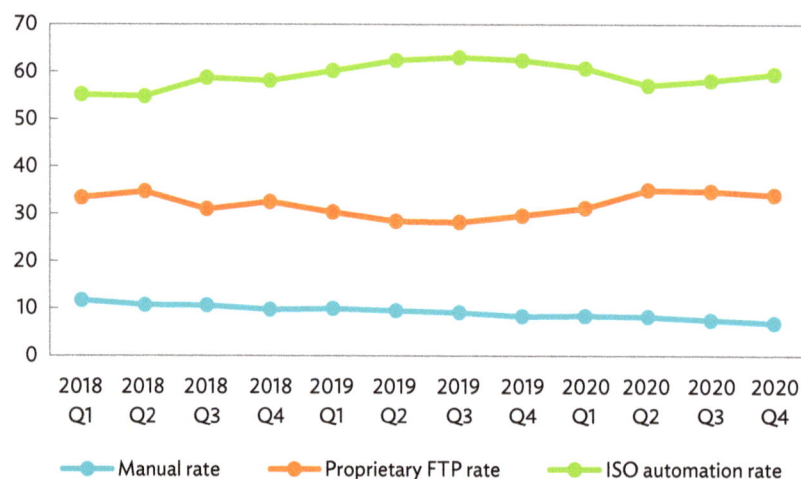

Figure 5: Total Fund Order Processing Rates, 2018–2020
(%)

ISO = International Organization for Standardization, Prop FTP = Proprietary File Transfer Protocol, Q = quarter.
Source: European Fund and Asset Management Association. 2021. *Fund Processing Standardisation Annual Report on Automation and Standardisation of Cross-Border Funds Orders in 2020.*

F.   Undertaking for Collective Investment in Transferable Securities Delivery versus Payment Scheme by TARGET2-Securities

Whenever investors subscribe to a CIS, new issue(s) should be released and the number of issued units changes accordingly, thus, necessitating extraordinary requirements on transaction processing, record keeping, and reconciliation when compared with other securities.

Although TARGET2-Securities (T2S) performs a wide range of settlement-related services including issuance, redemption, and corporate action processing, this report intends to focus on the delivery versus payment (DVP) settlement of subscription orders.

1. *Stakeholders for Undertaking for Collective Investment in Transferable Securities Collective Investment Scheme Settlement under TARGET2-Securities*

Investor

In CIS investing, investors can be categorized as follows:

- ▶ retail investor;
- ▶ institutional investor (e.g., a pension CIS, some other fund of funds, distributors, and insurance companies); and
- ▶ nominee (e.g., investor's custodian bank).

Investors may settle trades either directly or indirectly on T2S or with the transfer agent appointed by the CIS. To settle trades at the central securities depository (CSD) level or on T2S, retail or institutional investors need to open a securities account in a CSD on T2S (either in the issuer CSD or in the investor CSD for the respective security). Direct connectivity to T2S (e.g., for sending of instructions and receiving confirmations) is only available for investors that have reached an agreement for this with their CSD and have the necessary technical capacity.

An investor can be an ultimate beneficial owner, an intermediary to an ultimate beneficial owner, or an intermediary to another intermediary. In case that the investor is not the ultimate beneficial owner, every party in the transaction chain holds anti-money laundering and know-your-client (AML/KYC) responsibilities on their underlying clients. Every intermediary needs to ensure compliance with all AML/KYC regulations and give comfort to the entity where it holds securities account.

Central Securities Depository

The holdings of investors are kept either in segregated or collectively pooled accounts. CSD opens securities accounts for institutional investors who have signed an agreement with them to provide a neutral and scalable infrastructure for settlement (primary and secondary markets). There may also be multiple ancillary services offered by the CSD that are tailored for CIS, such as order routing, asset servicing, reconciliation, and reporting of trade-dated holdings.

The investor may hold CIS units directly with the issuer CSD. Alternatively, the investor may also hold CIS shares or via an investor CSD (which connects to the issuer CSD via a CSD link arrangement). The CSD of the investor authorizes and/or controls all orders and transfers issued by its participants and reconciles its records with statements transmitted by the issuing agent (issuing agent set-up) or issuer CSD (issuer CSD set-up).

AML/KYC checks on the investor CSDs are done by the issuer CSD, issuing agent, or by a transfer agent provided this is arranged for in the CSD link arrangement. For reasons of transparency, the investor CSD in most cases could provide disclosure reporting to the CIS manager of underlying holdings and transactions, either directly or indirectly through the issuer CSD, provided this is agreed with the CIS manager (e.g., the issuer for these securities).

The issuer CSD may also be the securities maintaining entity (SME), being responsible for creating and maintaining securities reference data in T2S.[23] T2S system specifications demand that each International Securities Identification Number (ISIN) has a single CSD fulfilling role of SME.

Issuing Agent

The issuing agent is an institution selected by the CIS manager to manage issuance of units and oversee settlement through T2S.

The issuing agent opens one or more issuance accounts in the issuer CSD on behalf of the CIS. The notary function is performed by the CSD. Depending on the future operating model of an asset manager, there may be multiple issuer CSDs and issuing agents connected to multiple investor CSDs.

The issuing agent shall obtain timely information whenever the transfer agent has updated a position on the transfer agent register following the execution of orders, transfers, and corporate actions. The issuing agent is required to transmit settlement instructions to the issuer CSD, reflecting all such register account updates, without undue delay.

Depending on the situation and preferences of the stakeholders, the issuing agent role can be assigned by the CIS manager to a local agent, a paying agent, or the transfer agent.

Transfer Agent

For each CIS, the asset manager must appoint a transfer agent to keep the register of all unitholders, within and outside of T2S. The transfer agent shall validate and execute the subscriptions, redemptions, switches, transfers, and corporate actions on the register accounts that result in the markup or markdown of shares owned by the account holder in a register.

In the context of T2S, the account holder in the register may be either the issuing agent or issuer CSD depending on the chosen set-up. The transfer agent must provide the owner with timely information of all relevant updates in the register.

Reports that the transfer agent produces include sums of registered and issued shares for the asset manager and CIS accountant, account statements for register account holders and distributors, and regulatory reporting. The transfer agent performs AML/KYC checks on the register account owner.

Securities Maintaining Entity

A Luxembourg CIS issued in a CSD will have had to provide the CSD with some static data, such as ISIN, name, and so forth. As for T2S, a list of securities should be provided. Maintenance data is to be maintained by the CSD bringing the (Luxembourg) CIS into T2S. An SME is defined as an entity, typically an issuer CSD, that has been assigned the responsibility for maintaining the reference data for a security in T2S.

In general, the CSD issuing a security is obliged to act in the SME role. Therefore, each participating CSD will be expected to maintain reference data in T2S for securities issued in its own market similar to

---

[23] Refer to Section 1.5.1.5 Securities Maintaining Entity for more details.

the current procedures. Additionally, a participating CSD may be assigned the SME role for a particular security for which it is not the issuer CSD.

The SME role entails various obligations for a CSD against the Eurosystem and other participating CSDs. Table 4 summarizes the obligations under the SME Framework Agreement for the sake of easy reference.

The SME is exclusively responsible for the creation and maintenance of four out of 11 data entities within the securities data management domain Table 5.

Table 4: Obligations under the Securities Maintaining Entity Framework Agreement

Obligations	Description
Creation Timeliness	The SME is responsible for creating reference data in a timely manner once a security is required for settlement.
Maintenance Continuation	The SME is responsible for the continuous maintenance of securities reference data once it has created a security (until the security is deleted or it has been agreed with other participating CSDs that the SME role is to be transferred to another CSD).
Correction Timeliness	The SME is responsible for correction of any errors or omissions within 2 hours once aware of this fact.
Securities Reference Data Rights	The SME is responsible for obtaining all authorizations, permits, and licenses to make available securities reference data in T2S.
Infringement of Third Party Rights	The SME is responsible for the reimbursement of all payments that the Eurosystem has to make to a third party due to an enforceable judgement related to the securities reference data introduced by the SME into T2S.
SME Role Reassignment	The SME is responsible for agreeing with another participating CSD to take over the SME role for a security and to inform Eurosystem in writing about the envisioned change in case that T2S shall reassign the responsibility on an exceptional basis.
Liability	The SME is liable for any errors or omissions in the reference data and responsible for settling any potential claims between the participating CSDs without involvement of the Eurosystem.

CSD = central securities depository, SME = securities maintaining entity, T2S = TARGET2-Securities.
Source: Q&A T2S for Fund Association of the Luxembourg Fund Industry.

Table 5: Securities Data Management under the Securities Maintaining Entity Framework

Securities Data Management		
Securities Maintaining Entity	Central Securities Depositories (including Securities Maintaining Entity)	National Central Banks and Payment Banks
• Securities	• Market-Specific	• Close Link
• Securities Code	• Security Attribute Value	• Securities Valuation
• Securities Name	• Security CSD Link	• Securities Valuation Party
• Deviating Settlement Unit	• Security Restriction	• Security Auto-Collateralization Eligibility

CSD = central securities depository.
Source: Q&A T2S for Fund Association of the Luxembourg Fund Industry.

2. *Authorization and Delivery versus Payment Settlement of Undertaking for Collective Investment in Transferable Securities Collective Investment Scheme*

Authorization of Undertaking for Collective Investment in Transferable Securities Collective Investment Scheme

UCITS CIS are authorized via the following procedures (Figure 6):

▶ Once established, a UCITS CIS should be authorized by the home economy regulator.

▶ The authorization should be notified to the corresponding host economy regulator.

▶ The home economy regulator should notify the CIS operator about the notification.

▶ Within 5 business days after the notification, the host economy regulator should notify the home economy regulator about the results of validation review on the UCITS CIS.

▶ After 10 business days since the completion of the procedure, the UCITS CIS can be distributed in the host economy.

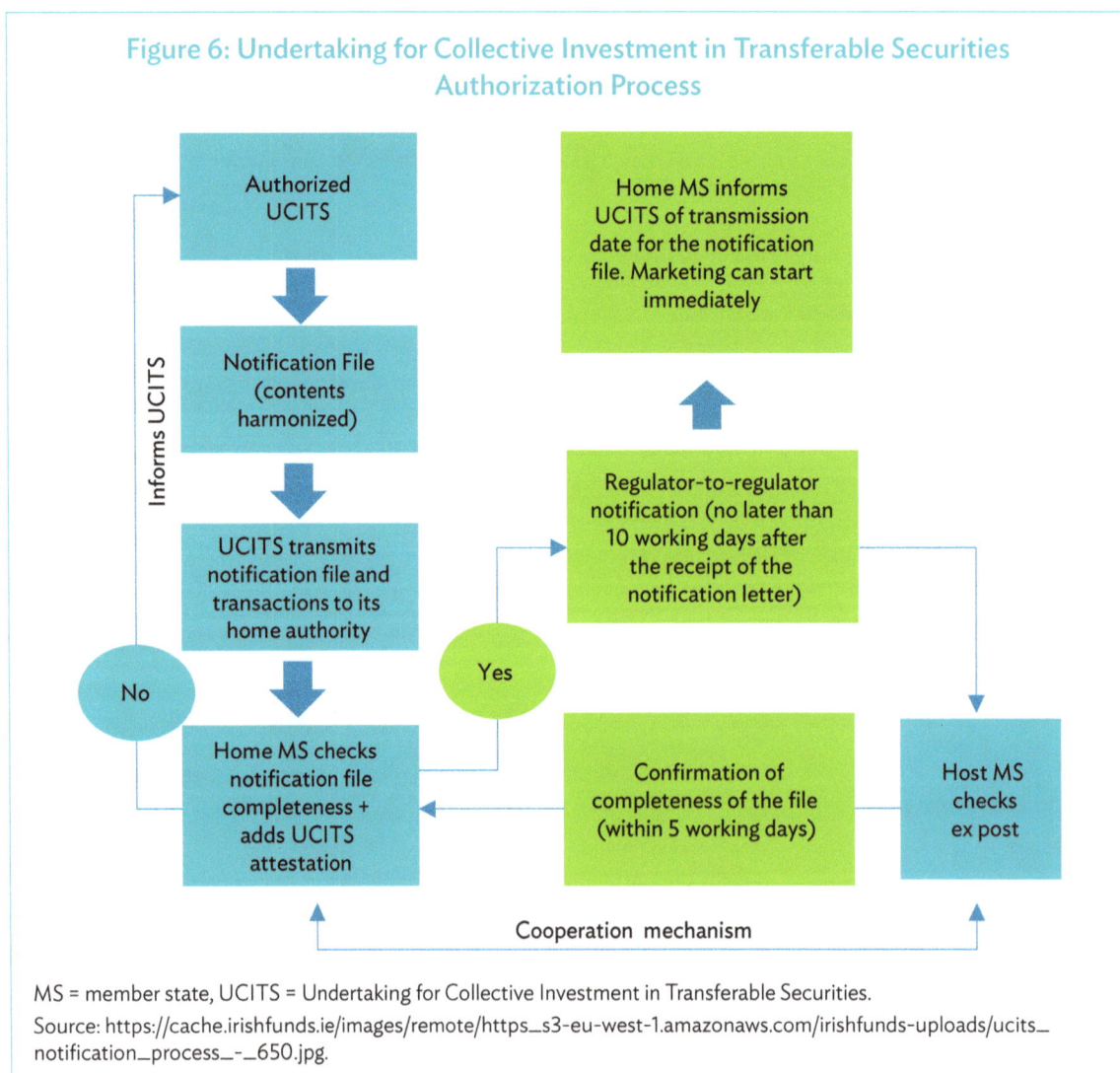

Figure 6: Undertaking for Collective Investment in Transferable Securities Authorization Process

MS = member state, UCITS = Undertaking for Collective Investment in Transferable Securities.
Source: https://cache.irishfunds.ie/images/remote/https_s3-eu-west-1.amazonaws.com/irishfunds-uploads/ucits_notification_process_-_650.jpg.

The home economy regulator has 10 working days from the receipt of the notification file to notify the host state regulator. The host economy regulator has at most 5 working days to confirm to the home state regulator that the notification file has been received and the documents are printable and readable.

Subscription of Undertaking for Collective Investment in Transferable Securities Collective Investment Scheme

Once a UCITS CIS is notified to the host economy, the investor can initiate subscription. For subscription, the investor should make payment to the bank designated by the asset manager, while the asset manager should deliver beneficiary certificates to the investor. Given the nature of UCITS, payment of cash and delivery of securities cross the borders of home and host economies.

If an investor subscribes to a CIS in France, Germany, or Switzerland, it is the local CSD that provides a platform for the processing of issuance, settlement, and corporate action. The relevant procedures are described in Figure 7.

Figure 7: Issuer Central Securities Depository Set-Up Order Processing of Undertaking for Collective Investment in Transferable Securities Collective Investment Scheme

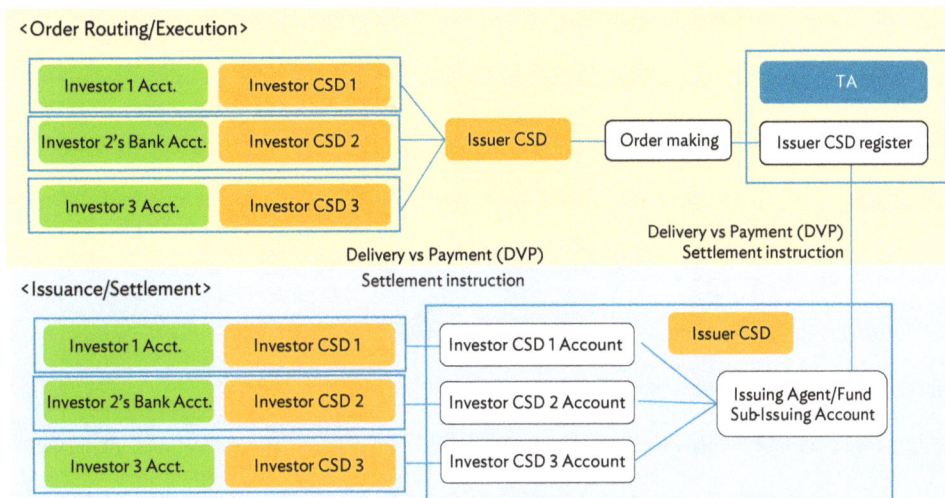

Acct. = account, CSD = central securities depository, TA = transfer agent.

Notes:
- Investor CSD is a CSD that holds a security for which it is not the/an Issuer CSD. It holds these securities either directly or indirectly via one or more intermediaries at the/an Issuer CSD.
- Issuer CSD is a CSD in which securities are issued (or immobilized). The issuer CSD opens accounts allowing investors (in a direct holding system) and/or intermediaries (including investor CSDs) to hold these securities.
- Issuing agent is an agent appointed by the fund to manage the issuance process and the creation or cancellation of fund shares in the fund issuance account.
- The CIS appoints the issuer CSD.
- The order for subscription or redemption is sent by the investor, either directly or through the chosen investor CSD, to the issuer CSD.
- The issuer CSD holds an account at the TA.
- The issuer CSD is the register of all CIS shareholders for shares issued/to be issued through TARGET2-Securities.
- The issuer CSD opens a settlement account with the TA that is also appointed by the asset manager.

Source: Association of the Luxembourg Fund Industry. 2016. Q&A Target2-Securities for Fund (Updated). Luxembourg.

The issuing agent set-up depicted in Figure 8 has been adopted by Luxembourg and Ireland, and is typically processed via the contact between distributor and transfer agent.

Figure 8: Issuing Agent Set-Up Order Processing of Undertaking for Collective Investment in Transferable Securities Collective Investment Scheme

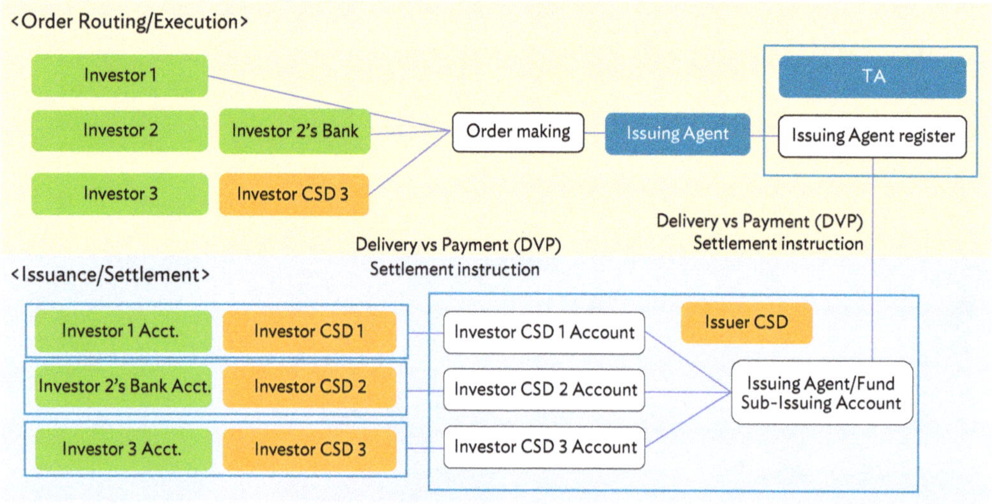

Acct. = account, CSD = central securities depository, TA = transfer agent.
Notes:
- Investor CSD is a CSD that holds a security for which it is not the issuer CSD. It holds these securities either directly or indirectly via one or more intermediaries at the/an Issuer CSD.
- Issuer CSD is a CSD in which securities are issued (or immobilized). The issuer CSD opens accounts allowing investors (in a direct holding system) and/or intermediaries (including investor CSDs) to hold these securities.
- Issuing agent is an agent appointed by the fund to manage the issuance process and the creation or cancellation of fund shares in the fund issuance account.
- The CIS appoints the issuing agent.
- The order for subscription or redemption is sent by the investor, either directly or through the chosen investor CSD, to the issuing agent.
- The issuing agent holds an account at the TA.
- The issuing agent is the register of all CIS shareholders for shares issued/to be issued through TARGET2-Securities.
- The issuing agent opens a settlement account with the issuer CSD that is also appointed by the asset manager.
Source: Association of the Luxembourg Fund Industry. 2016. Q&A Target2-Securities for Fund (Updated). Luxembourg.

Delivery versus Payment Settlement of Undertaking for Collective Investment in Transferable Securities Collective Investment Scheme via TARGET2-Securities

Luxembourg-domiciled CIS are eligible in Clearstream Germany, Euroclear France, LuxCSD, and VP LUX; these platforms all use central bank money today for settling EUR-denominated transactions. Clearstream Bank Germany performs settlement in central bank money through the Ancillary System Interface procedures, which allows the use of accounts in TARGET2-Securities (T2S) held with any euro area central bank.

LuxCSD performs settlement in central bank money through the Ancillary System Interface procedure, which allows the use of accounts in TARGET2 held with any euro area central bank. Euroclear France, as the French CSD, uses central bank money. The real-time settlement for UCITS subscription is demonstrated by the flowchart in Figure 9.

Figure 9: Delivery versus Payment Settlement of Undertaking for Collective Investment in Transferable Securities Collective Investment Scheme via TARGET2-Securities

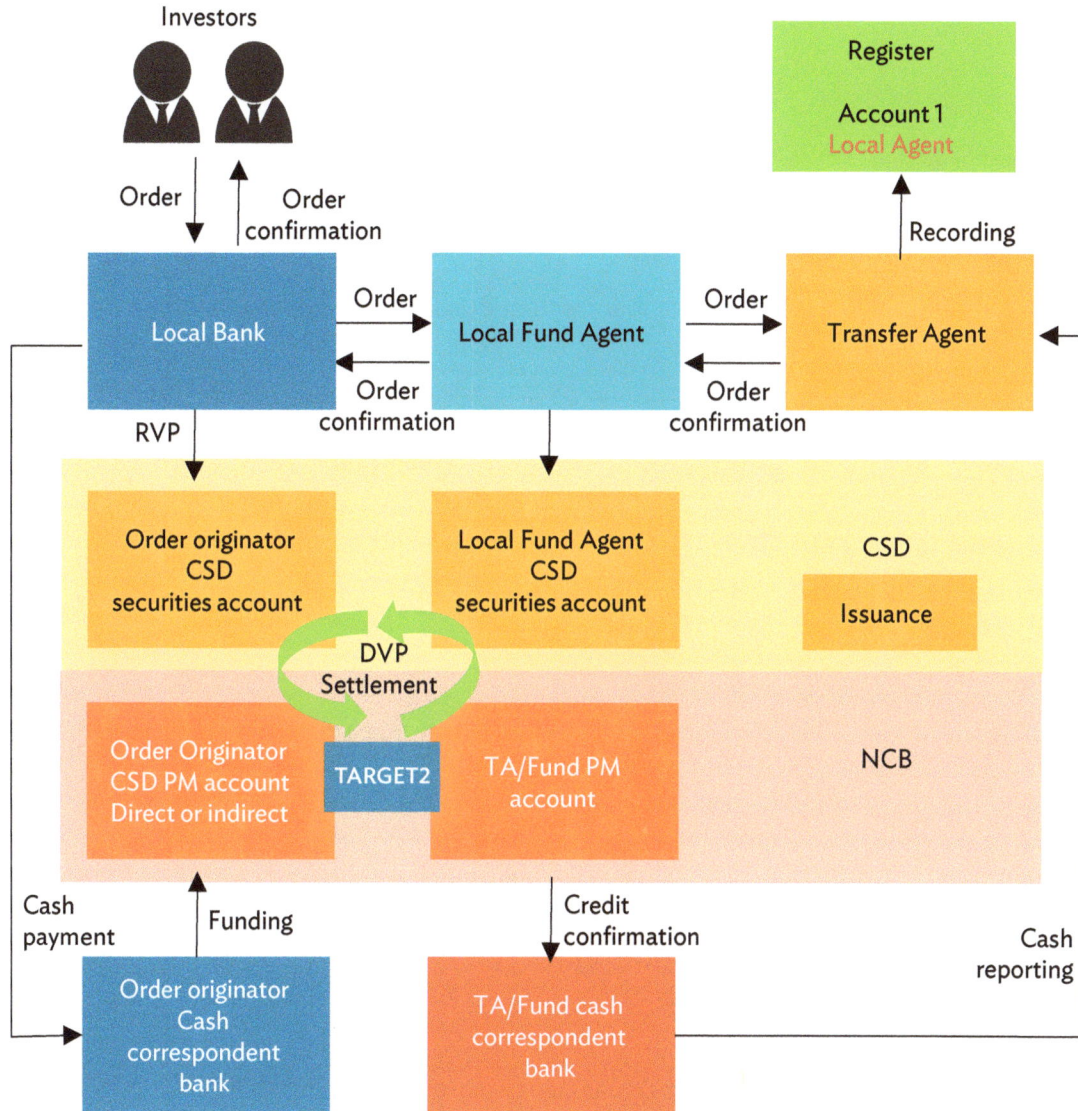

CSD = central securities depository, DVP = delivery versus payment, NCB = national central bank, PM = payment module, RVP = receive versus payment, TA = transfer agent.

Notes:
- Receive versus payment is a simultaneous exchange of securities against cash.
- Payment module account means an account held by a TARGET2 participant in the PM with a central bank, which is necessary for such TARGET2 participants.
- Order originator means order giver or sender of an investment funds order (subscription, redemption, or switch).
- An NCB is the central bank of a sovereign state; the European Central Bank is not an NCB. The quality of cash held at an NCB is similar to central bank money.

Source: Association of the Luxembourg Fund Industry. 2016. Q&A Target2-Securities for Fund (Updated). Luxembourg.

G.   Completeness, Finality, and Irrevocability of Undertaking for Collective Investment in Transferable Securities Collective Investment Scheme Settlement

1.   Central Securities Depository Regulation

The Central Securities Depositories Regulation (CSDR), which entered into force on 17 September 2014, was promulgated by the European Parliament and the European Council in a quest to enhance the pan-European capital market settlement.

Settlement is meant to finalize the corresponding rights and obligations of transaction parties. CIS transaction settlement is subject to the rights and obligations stated in Table 6.

Table 6: Rights and Obligations to Be Settled

	Rights	**Obligations**
Home Economy	Cash to receive	Securities to issue and deliver
	[Responsible Entity] • Asset management company • Custodian • Depositary or TA (NAV calculation)	[Responsible Entity] • Depositary or TA
Host Economy	Securities to receive (in physical form or in the form of rights)	Cash to pay
	[Responsible Entity] • Distributor	[Responsible Entity] • Custodian

NAV = net asset value, TA = transfer agent.
Note: A depositary is a financial institution that is appointed under a collective investment scheme (fund's) constitution to oversee the operation of the fund and to whom its assets are entrusted for safekeeping.
Source: ADB compilation.

There are three key elements that constitute the settlement of the aforementioned rights and obligations: completeness, finality, and irrevocability.

Settlement completeness refers to the procedural completion of settlement in accordance with transaction terms and conditions. Settlement is complete once the trade goes through the confirmation of settlement data, the execution of DVP settlement, the recording of beneficial ownership, and the payment of cash.

CSDR provides that transfer orders entered into securities settlement systems in accordance with the rules of those systems should be legally enforceable and binding on third parties. It is also required by CSDR that CSDs should define the moment or moments when transfer orders are entered into their systems and become irrevocable.

In addition, in order to secure legal certainty, CSDs should disclose to their participants at the moment when the transfer of securities and cash in a securities settlement system is legally enforceable and binding on third parties in accordance, as the case may be, with national law. CSDs should also take all reasonable measures to ensure that transfers of securities and cash are legally enforceable and binding on third parties no later than at the end of the business day of the actual settlement date.

CSDR also requires that the delivery of securities be represented in book-entry form regardless of issuance type and that the settlement be executed in the economy where the securities are issued.[24] It is prescribed in Article 39.7 of CSDR that all securities transactions against cash between direct participants in a Securities Settlement System (SSS) operated by a CSD and settled in that SSS shall be settled on a DVP basis.

Article 40.1 of CSDR states that for transactions denominated in the currency of the country where the settlement takes place, a CSD shall settle the cash payments of its SSS through accounts opened with a central bank of issue of the relevant currency where practical and available.

DVP settlement is reflected in the record of beneficial ownership via the corresponding changes of the cash and securities positions of both buyers and sellers. What matters here is that such beneficial ownership recording should be legally enforceable and binding in strict accordance with investor rights and obligations. The legality of beneficial ownership recording is described in the 11th clause in the preamble of CSDR.[25]

2. *Settlement Finality in Payment and Securities Settlement Systems*

As mentioned above, settlement also goes hand in hand with finality and irrevocability. Even after DVP settlement, there is still a possibility of settlement cancellation as in the case of the insolvency of a counterparty.

For the prevention of settlement cancellation, the European Union (EU) adopted Directive 98/26/EC of the European Parliament and of the Council on Settlement Finality in Payment and Securities Settlement Systems. The directive laid a solid foundation for preventing or minimizing the settlement failures of central bank's RTGS system and CSD-run SSS. The directive governs not only the domestic transaction of EU member states but also cross-border transactions among member states.[26]

The directive prescribes that EU member states should clearly define in their local laws and regulations the scope of settlement finality (e.g., applicable participants, systems on clearing, settlement, or collateral management, and type of transaction).[27] The systems designated for settlement finality are legally applicable to not only direct participants but also indirect participants and other relevant third

---

[24] Refer to Article 4.1 of CSDR.

[25] Such securities should be recorded in a CSD book-entry system in order to ensure, inter alia, that all such securities can be settled in a securities settlement system. Immobilization and dematerialization should not imply any loss of rights for the holders of securities and should be achieved in a way that ensures that holders of securities can verify their rights.

[26] Directive 98/26/EC (6).

[27] Directive 98/26/EC Article 1 (a), Article 2 (a), Article 10.

parties. Once submitted to such systems, trade-related instructions are irrevocable.[28] Any settlement therein cannot be canceled,[29] even in the case where a counterparty is insolvent.[30]

H. Characteristics of Undertaking for Collective Investment in Transferable Securities as a Collective Investment Scheme Passport

1. Focus on Public Open-End Collective Investment Scheme for Authorization[31]

One of the key recipes for the success of UCITS was the emphasis on investor protection and the transparency of CIS management. Closed-end CIS were excluded from the scope of UCITS because open-end CIS were deemed to provide better protection for retail investors who may not be financially sophisticated enough to handle complex and risky products.

The redemption of closed-end CIS is much more costly than open-end ones since closed-end CIS are usually formed in the structure of an investment company, which is not redeemable unless listed on a regulated market. In other words, offshore investors residing in a host economy should endure the hassle of having to engage in cross-border transaction in the regulated market of the home economy in order to redeem their units.

Meanwhile, open-end CIS can be redeemed at the distributor level, thus, exposed to less risks and allowing for more liquidity than closed-end CIS.[32] Such differences in the nature of open-end and closed-end CIS are well described in UCITS.[33] Unlike open-end ones, closed-end CIS tend to be opaque in terms of the fairness of market pricing and clarity of disclosure.[34]

2. Expansion of Collective Investment Scheme Passporting Schemes

UCITS was established in 1985 to allow for passporting schemes that facilitate the free flow of CIS. Since then, the EU has continued to drive deregulatory policies to reduce transaction costs and boost efficiencies by improving the UCITS transaction experience. A notable case in point would be the passporting schemes for management companies and depositaries, which contributed much to helping the regional industry to achieve substantial economies of scale.[35]

---

[28] Directive 98/26/EC (14).

[29] Directive 98/26/EC Article 5. A transfer order may not be revoked by a participant in a system, nor by a third party, from the moment defined by the rules of that system.

[30] Insolvency proceedings shall not have retroactive effects on the rights and obligations of a participant arising from, or in connection with, its participation in a system earlier than the moment of opening of such proceedings as defined in Article 6(1).

[31] Article 3(a), (b) of UCITS.

[32] This was quoted from an interview with an asset management company in Luxembourg.

[33] It is desirable to permit a UCITS to invest its assets in units of UCITS and other collective investment undertakings of the open-end type that also invest in liquid financial assets referred to in UCITS and which operate on the principle of risk spreading. It is necessary that UCITS or other collective investment undertakings in which a UCITS invests be subject to effective supervision.

[34] CIS are mostly valued based on the assets included in the CIS basket. However, a closed-end CIS may be valued differently from the value of the net assets included since the value of a closed-end CIS is determined in a market where it is listed.

[35] The concept of ManCo passporting is included in UCITS IV (launched in 2009), while the passporting scheme for depositaries is expected to be addressed in the forthcoming UCITS VI and executed accordingly.

Role of Management Company[36]

UCITS are required either to be self-managed or appointed by a management company (ManCo). The ManCo is ultimately responsible for the operations of the UCITS and most of its functions, but will generally delegate most tasks to more efficiently conduct business (e.g., portfolio management, administration, marketing, and distribution). There must be clear monitoring activities and management functions that take place at the ManCo level, and often requirements exist to have employees physically based and residing in the country of domicile of the ManCo. Self-managed CIS are not required to appoint a ManCo but can do so.

Role of Depositary[37]

The role of a European depositary bank is similar to what the custodian of a US mutual fund performs. Plus, there are strict criteria in each domicile governing the types of entities that are eligible to act as a depositary. Most national laws mandate that only credit institutions located in the country of domiciliation or a branch of an EU credit institution may be appointed as depositary.

Additionally, the duties and responsibilities of a UCITS depositary bank are much more extensive than those of a US mutual fund's custodian. In addition to the safekeeping of the UCITS' assets, the depositary bank also has additional oversight duties, including ensuring the following:

▶ subscriptions and redemptions of shares or units are carried out in accordance with the offering documents;

▶ all considerations, in relation to transactions involving any assets of the CIS, are remitted within usual time limits; and

▶ the application of CIS income is appropriate and in accordance with the offering documents.

I.   Implications

First, despite its ambitious vision for the future of the European asset management industry, the 1985 debut of UCITS was initially faced with a lukewarm market reception. The EU attributed this to the lack of standardization frameworks for the pan-European single market. One of the policy recommendations was to promote the harmonization of settlement and other post-trade processing for cross-border transaction in Europe. It is noteworthy that Europe viewed settlement not as back-office plumbing but as one of the crucial game changers for the betterment of market efficiency.

Second, the pan-European settlement reform trickled down from the top with the right balance of roles and responsibilities and division of work. The overall direction and guideline of relevant policies were determined by the EC.

---

[36] A UCITS management company refers to a management company as defined in Council Directive 85/611/EEC of 20 December 1985, on the coordination of laws, regulations, and administrative provisions relating to undertakings for collective investment in transferable securities.

[37] A depositary refers to an institution entrusted with the duties set out in Articles 22 and 32 and subject to the other provisions laid down in Chapter IV and Section 3 of Chapter V of UCITS.

The working-level frameworks for industry standardization were built by FPSG, which was established by EFAMA. Such concerted efforts culminated in the successful launch of T2S—a regional settlement platform run by the European Central Bank and having onboarded European CSDs and central banks. The long journey of settlement reform was carefully approached with a holistic perspective in consideration of general post-trade harmonization.

Also, the EU bolstered regulatory frameworks on settlement finality so that the settlement of every securities trade in Europe (including UCITS fund transaction and intra-regional cross-border transaction) is free from being revoked once such settlement is finalized.

ASIAN COLLECTIVE INVESTMENT SCHEME MARKET AND PASSPORTS

Many experts estimate that the growth potential of the Asian fund market is very large because the size of the collective investment scheme (CIS) market in Asia is only a quarter of that of the United States (US) and one-half that of Europe, although there is not too much difference in the size of regional gross domestic products (GDPs) (Figure 10).

Figure 10: Asia Collective Investment Scheme Market versus the United States and Europe
(USD trillion)

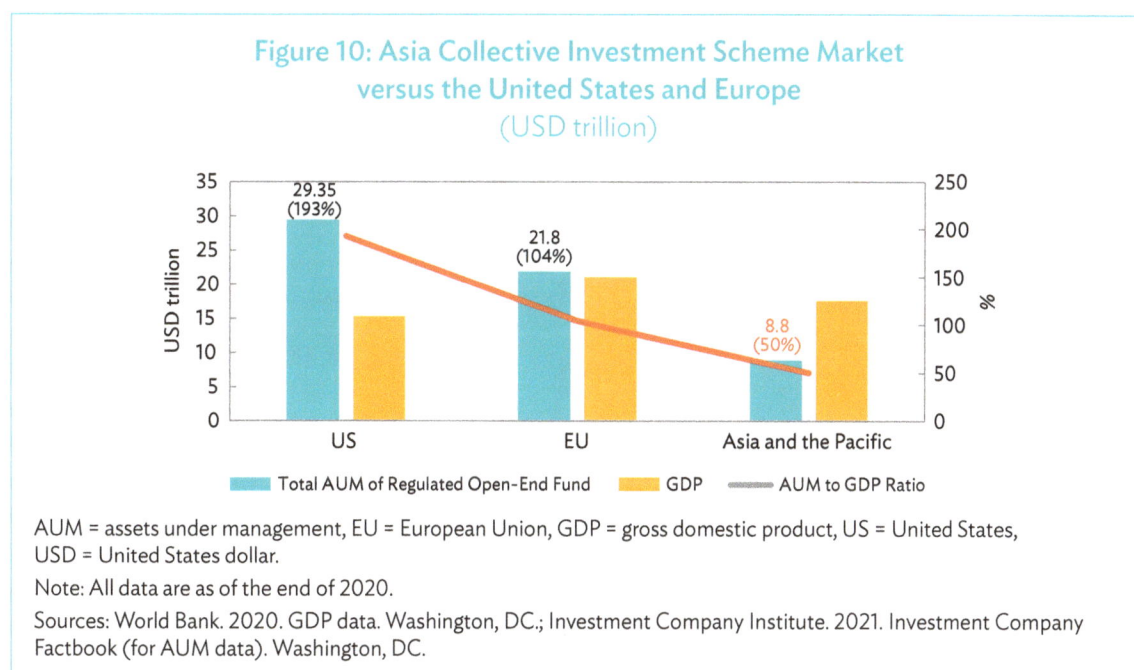

AUM = assets under management, EU = European Union, GDP = gross domestic product, US = United States, USD = United States dollar.
Note: All data are as of the end of 2020.
Sources: World Bank. 2020. GDP data. Washington, DC.; Investment Company Institute. 2021. Investment Company Factbook (for AUM data). Washington, DC.

The Asia and Pacific region (8.8%) ranked fourth in the share of total net assets of worldwide regulated open-end funds at the end of 2020. For the number of established CIS (28%), it ranked second, following only Europe (46%) (Figures 11 and 12).

This section describes the current status of ASEAN+3 CIS markets based on the results of a survey conducted among member states and the findings of additional investigations.

Due to the constraints of this research, the scope of the survey was effectively narrowed to CIS cross-border transactions, the operation of a central processing platform, settlement models, market characteristics, and other details, as of the end of 2020, with a particular focus on post-trade infrastructure (e.g., settlement procedures and central processing platform for subscription and redemption).

The later sections of this chapter describe the key survey findings about ASEAN+3 economies. Other detailed information is presented by economy in Appendix 1: Overview of ASEAN+3 CIS Markets.

Figure 11: Share of Total Net Assets of Worldwide Regulated Open-End Funds
(USD trillion)

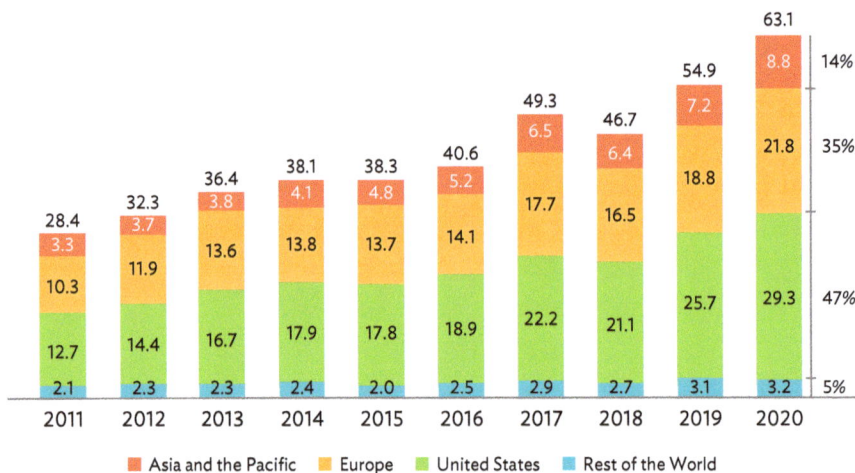

USD = United States dollar.

Notes: Regulated open-end collective investment scheme (CIS) include mutual funds, exchange-traded funds, and institutional CIS. All data are as of the end of 2020.

Source: Investment Company Institute. 2021. *Investment Company Fact Book*. Washington, DC.

Figure 12: Number of Worldwide Regulated Open-End Funds

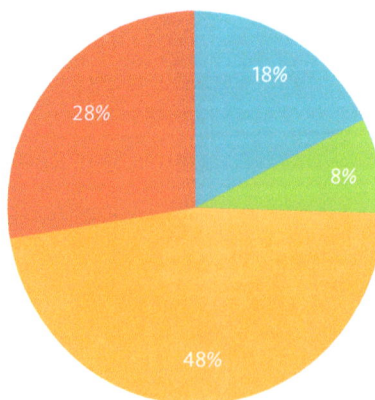

Total number of worldwide regulated open-end funds: 126,457

■ Asia and the Pacific ■ Europe ■ United States ■ Rest of the World

Notes: Regulated open-end collective investment scheme (CIS) include mutual funds, exchange-traded funds, and institutional CIS. All data are as of the end of 2020.

Source: Investment Company Institute. 2021. *Investment Company Fact Book*. Washington, DC.

A.   Overview of Cross-Border Transactions in ASEAN+3 Economies

1.   ASEAN+3 Economies' Cross-Border Collective Investment Scheme Distribution

Table 7 demonstrates the current status of inbound and outbound transaction of CIS in ASEAN+3 economies.

As shown in Table 7, most ASEAN+3 economies seem to have opened up for cross-border transactions. However, it was found that some economies had trouble engaging in actual inbound or outbound transactions due to differing views on tax neutrality, corporate action processing, and other working-level issues.

Table 7: ASEAN+3 Cross-Border Collective Investment Scheme Distribution

Economies	Outbound Transaction (Home-Domiciled Collective Investment Scheme Sold Abroad)	Inbound Transaction (Foreign Collective Investment Scheme Sold at Home)
Brunei Darussalam	No	Yes
People's Republic of China	No Answer (There should exist both northbound and southbound transaction between the People's Republic of China and Hong Kong, China given the implementation of MRF.)	
Cambodia	N.A.	
Indonesia	Yes	Yes
Republic of Korea	Yes	Yes
Japan	Yes	Yes
Lao PDR	Yes	No Answer
Hong Kong, China	Yes	Yes
Malaysia	Yes	Yes
Philippines	No	Yes
Singapore	Yes	Yes
Thailand	Yes	No
Viet Nam	No	No

ASEAN+3 = Association of Southeast Asian Nations plus the People's Republic of China, Japan, and the Republic of Korea; Lao PDR = Lao People's Democratic Republic; MRF= Mutual Recognition of Funds; N.A. = not applicable.
Note: All information is as of the end of 2020.
Source: ADB Cross-Border Settlement Infrastructure Forum (CSIF) Survey.

2. ASEAN+3 Economies' Central Platform

The complex processes and numerous stakeholders of CIS were discussed earlier in this report. Many economies around the world have built and run a central platform for more efficient processing of CIS-related post-trade operations. In general, CIS markets can be classified into three models: central securities depository (CSD) model, transfer agent model, and international CSD (ICSD) model (Figure 13).[38]

The CSD model refers to a market where post-trade operations are mainly processed by a CSD-run central platform while the transfer agent model is a market formed by multiple transfer agents with a weaker role played by a CSD. As for ICSD model, the cross-border transaction of Undertaking for Collective Investment in Transferable Securities (UCITS) CIS is supported by the platform of ICSDs, such as FundSettle of Euroclear and Vestima of Clearstream.

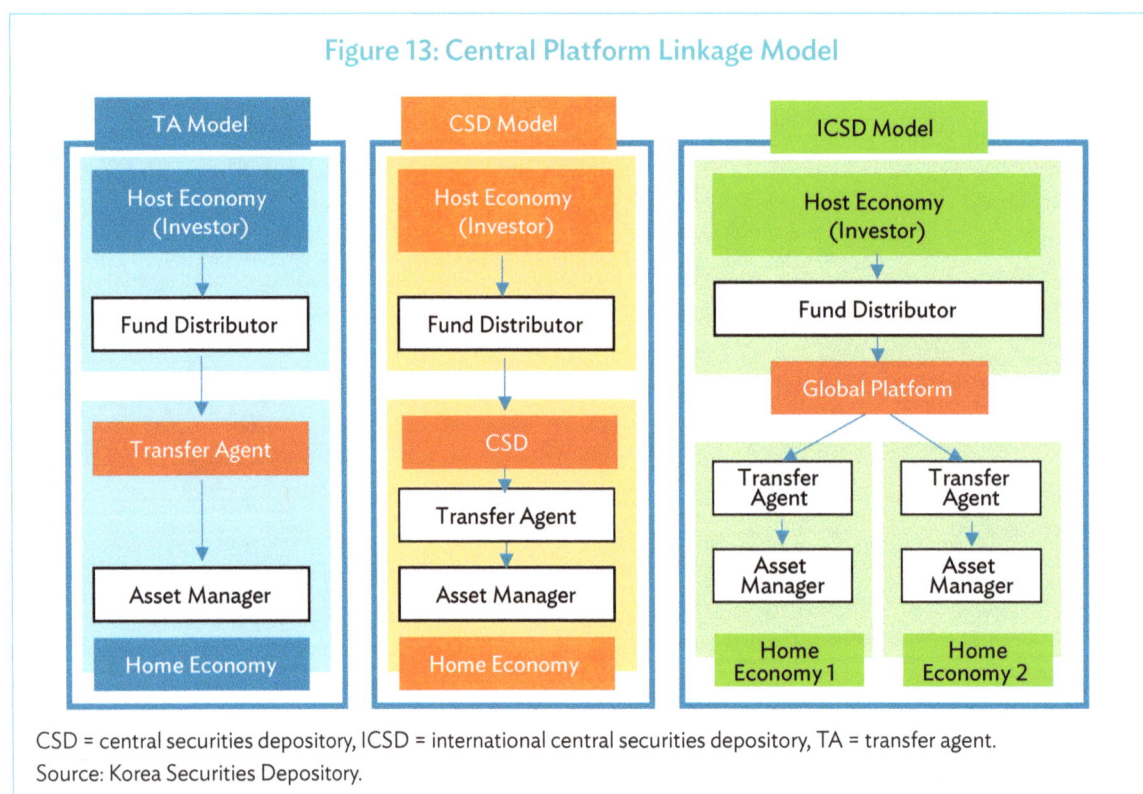

Figure 13: Central Platform Linkage Model

CSD = central securities depository, ICSD = international central securities depository, TA = transfer agent.
Source: Korea Securities Depository.

Central Securities Depository Model

The CSD model requires a CSD to establish a central platform to process orders (for subscription and redemption), settlement, or other operations. On the same platform, the distributor routes orders to the asset manager who in turn places a settlement instruction to the custodian. Based on the instruction,

---

[38] The divide between CSD, ICSD, and transfer agent models is merely a theoretical categorization for easy understanding. Actual markets may take a hybrid form of either or all of the models mentioned herein.

the custodian settles the cash and units. The entire process takes place on the platform in a delivery versus payment (DVP) manner. Depending on economies, central platforms may be customized either to electronic registration or to a conventional deposit and settlement system. Within ASEAN+3, the CSD model has been adopted by Indonesia, Japan, the Republic of Korea, Thailand, and Viet Nam.

Transfer Agent Model

The transfer agent model requires transfer agents designated by asset management companies to process the entire operation for subscription and redemption (Figure 14). The distributor in this model opens a cash account and a securities account with the transfer agent and routes orders. The transfer agent carries out settlement with the custodian, as well as register keeping, reporting, and other administrative operations. The transfer agent model has been adopted by the People's Republic of China; the EU; Hong Kong, China; and Singapore.[39]

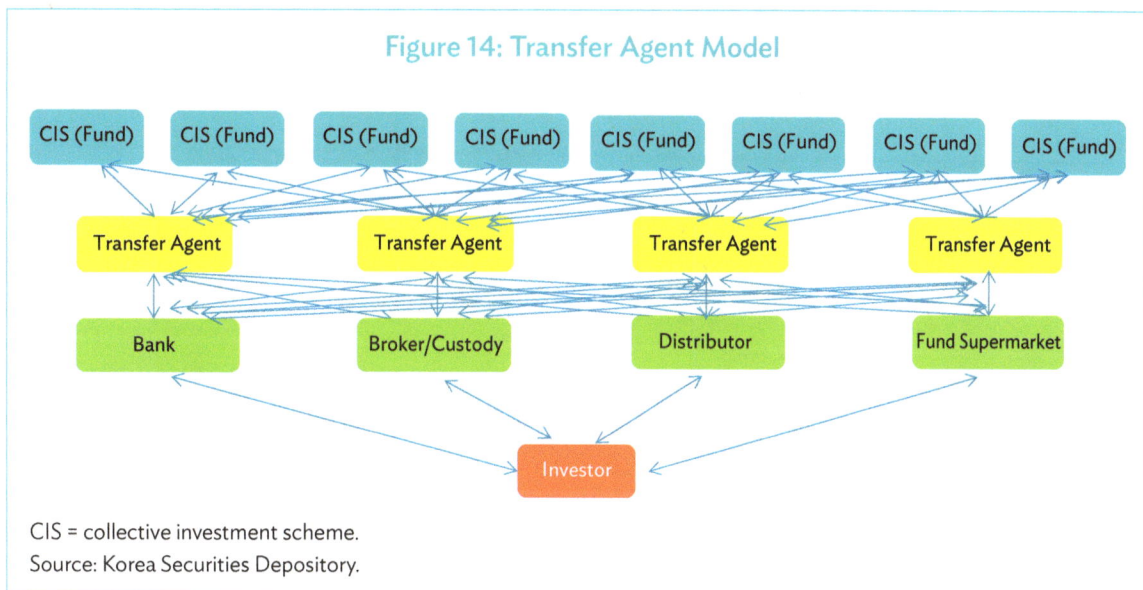

Figure 14: Transfer Agent Model

CIS = collective investment scheme.
Source: Korea Securities Depository.

International Central Securities Depository Model

As one of the internationally recognized CIS passport brands, UCITS involves distributors, asset managers, and custodians operating in different jurisdictions that are mostly connected via ICSD platforms, such as FundSettle of Euroclear and Vestima of Clearstream.

FundSettle and Vestima offer straight-through-processing (STP) solutions to connect distributors in the host economy with the custodians, CSDs, transfer agents, and asset managers in the home economy.

---

[39] The economies were categorized by model based on the Asian Development Bank Cross-Border Settlement Infrastructure Forum (ADB CSIF) survey and Asia Fund Standardization Forum (AFSF) reports.

Table 8: Central Platform of ASEAN+3 Economies

Economies	Name of Central Platform	Operator	Model	International Central Securities Depository Linkage
Brunei Darussalam	There is no central platform.			
People's Republic of China	Central Data Exchange Platform (CDEP)	CSDC	TA Model	
Cambodia	There is no central platform.			
Indonesia	S-INVEST	KSEI	CSD Model	
Republic of Korea	FundNet	KSD	CSD Model	Euroclear Clearstream
Japan	Private Vendor Financial Network System	Investment Trust Industry	CSD Model	
Lao PDR	There is no central platform.			
Hong Kong, China	CMU Fund Order Routing and Settlement Service	HKMA	TA Model	Euroclear Clearstream
Malaysia	There is no central platform.			
Philippines	There is no central platform.			
Singapore	–	–	TA Model	
Thailand	FundConnext	SET	CSD Model	Clearstream
Viet Nam	Open-ended Fund Management System and ETFs System	VSD	CSD Model	

– = none, CMU = Central Moneymarkets Unit, CSD = central securities depository, CSDC = China Securities Depository and Clearing Corporation, ETF = exchange-traded funds, HKMA = Hong Kong Monetary Authority, KSD = Korea Securities Depository, KSEI = PT Kustodian Sentral Efek Indonesia (Indonesia Central Securities Depository), Lao PDR = Lao People's Democratic Republic, SET = Stock Exchange of Thailand, TA = transfer agent, VSD = Vietnam Securities Depository.
Note: Information is as of the end of 2020.
Source: ADB Cross-Border Settlement Infrastructure Forum (CSIF) Survey.

3.   *Collective Investment Scheme Settlement Model and Completeness and Finality of Settlement*

Given its "exchange-of-value" nature, CIS subscription and redemption involve linked obligations and should be settled on a DVP manner in order to eliminate principal risks. This section of the report describes the current status of CIS settlement in the ASEAN+3 region.

Table 9: Delivery versus Payment Settlement of Collective Investment Scheme in ASEAN+3

Economies	Delivery versus Payment Settlement via Central Securities Depository–Central Bank Linkage
Brunei Darussalam	No
Cambodia	No
People's Republic of China	No Answer
Hong Kong, China	No
Indonesia	Yes (Linkage between S-INVEST and BI-RTGS)
Japan	Yes (Linkage between BETS and BOJ-Wire)
Republic of Korea	Yes (Linkage between FundNet and BOK-Wire)
Lao PDR	No
Malaysia	No
Philippines	No
Singapore	No
Thailand	No
Viet Nam	No

ASEAN+3 = Association of Southeast Asian Nations plus the People's Republic of China, Japan, and the Republic of Korea; BETS = Book-Entry Transfer System; BI-RTGS= Bank Indonesia Real Time Gross Settlement System; BOJ = Bank of Japan; BOK = Bank of Korea; Lao PDR = Lao People's Democratic Republic.
Note: Information is as of the end of 2020.
Source: ADB Cross-Border Settlement Infrastructure Forum (CSIF) Survey.

B.   Asia Region Funds Passport

1.   Outline

Initially proposed by Australia in the Australian Financial Centre Forum in 2010 and further discussed through the Asia-Pacific Economic Cooperation Finance Ministers' Process, the Asia Region Funds Passport (ARFP) has established itself as a multilateral framework intended to support the development of the Asia CIS industry through improved market access and regulatory harmonization.[40]

In 2016, representatives from the governments of Australia, Japan, New Zealand, the Republic of Korea, and Thailand signed a memorandum of cooperation that came into effect on 30 June 2016 with the following key objectives (Table 10):

▶ Providing investors in the economy of each of the participants with a more diverse range of investment opportunities, enabling them to better manage their portfolio and meet their investment objectives;

▶ Deepening the region's capital markets to attract finance for economic growth in the region;

▶ Facilitating the recycling of the region's savings locally, growing the pool of funds available for investment in the region;

---

[40]   See https://fundspassport.apec.org.

▶ Strengthening the capacity, expertise, and international competitiveness of financial markets in the region and the CIS industry, with a view to supporting sound economic development; and

▶ Maintaining the legal and regulatory frameworks that promote investor protection and fair, efficient, and transparent markets for financial services; supporting financial stability and providing high standards in the management and distribution of CIS.

Table 10: Progress of Asia Region Funds Passport

Timeline	Event
Sep 2013	At the 2013 APEC Finance Ministers' Meeting, finance ministers from Australia, the Republic of Korea, New Zealand, and Singapore signed a statement of intent in Bali, Indonesia on ARFP.
Sep 2015	Finance ministers from Australia, Japan, the Republic of Korea, New Zealand, the Philippines, and Thailand signed a statement of understanding at the APEC Finance Ministers' Meeting in Cebu, Philippines on ARFP.
Apr 2016	Australia, Japan, the Republic of Korea, and New Zealand signed a memorandum of cooperation.
May 2016	Thailand signed the memorandum of cooperation.
Feb 2019	ARFP went live with Australia, Japan, and Thailand and was ready to receive registration applications from local prospective passport CIS and entry applications from foreign passport CIS.
Jul 2019	Following the competition of regulatory arrangements, ARFP went live in New Zealand.
Dec 2019	Following the competition of regulatory arrangements, ARFP went live in the Republic of Korea.

APEC = Asia-Pacific Economic Cooperation, ARFP = Asia Region Funds Passport, CIS = collective investment scheme.
Source: Asia-Pacific Economic Cooperation. https://fundspassport.apec.org.

The fundamental principles for ARPF can be summed up as investor protection, legal and regulatory certainty, and global competitiveness (Table 11).

Table 11: Fundamental Principles of Asia Region Funds Passport

Principle	Details
Investor Protection	• Investor protection is the most important value given that ARFP CIS are confined to open-end public CIS. • ARPF CIS should be standardized enough to offer secure and reliable transaction experience to retail investors. • The ARFP framework imposes strict requirements on asset management companies, asset managers, concentration limits, distribution, and disclosure.
Legal and Regulatory Certainty	• The ARFP framework pursues legal and regulatory certainty based on the consensus of signatories with consideration of national differences. • ARPF CIS are registered via streamlined processes. • The ARFP framework puts forth cooperative measures for the regulators in both home and host economy.
Global Competitiveness	• ARFP is designed to stand as a highly recognized brand to replace UCITS. • While having an enlargement plan to expand its scope, ARFP is currently confined to economies with a high level of regulatory preparedness. • The ARFP framework was formulated in consideration of prior examples (e.g., UCITS, ASEAN CIS).

ARFP = Asia Region Funds Passport, ASEAN = Association of Southeast Asian Nations, ASEAN CIS = ASEAN collective investment schemes, UCITS = Undertaking for Collective Investment in Transferable Securities.
Source: Asia-Pacific Economic Cooperation. https://fundspassport.apec.org.

2. Architecture of Asia Region Funds Passport Memorandum of Cooperation

The memorandum of cooperation of ARFP comprises a preamble, 16 paragraphs, and 4 annexes. The preamble and the 16 paragraphs of main text describe the mutual agreements and general principles on the purpose and commitments of the passport, passport arrangements, participant eligibility, the set-up and role of joint committees, periodic progress reports, resolution of differences, and memorandum of commitment amendments:

▶ Annex 1 (Host Economy Laws and Regulations) sets out the applicable scope of host economy laws and regulations with regard to CIS names, disclosure, periodic reports, distribution.

▶ Annex 2 (Common Regulatory Arrangements) explains passport registration; notification; deregistration; winding up; asset management company requirements; the register of passport CIS; supervisory, investigative, administrative powers; and exemptions and modifications.

▶ Annex 3 (Passport Rules) prescribes the rules and requirements for passport CIS and operators, offerings, and portfolio allocation.

▶ Annex 4 (Cross-Border Supervisory Cooperation) states the cooperation among regulators, execution of requests for assistance, uses of information and consent, confidentiality of information, and onward sharing.

Key regulatory resources can be found in the official website of ARFP.[41] The basic structure of ARFP CIS resembles that of UCITS CIS (Table 12).

Table 12: Architecture of the Asia Region Funds Passport

Item	Basic Structure	Note
Target CIS	• Open-end public CIS	• ARFP CIS should be registered in and supervised by the home economy. • Permitted assets include securities and short-term financing products.
Registration	• Passport CIS registration in home economy • Notification to host economy and initiation of distribution	• The home economy is authorized to approve or disapprove the passport CIS registration.
Distribution	• Subject to host economy laws and regulations	• Distribution activities that have a huge impact on investor protection (such as disclosure) should be regulated by the pertinent laws of the host economy.
Supervision and Restriction	• Subject to both home and host economy	• Deregistration, or suspension of distribution, occurs when a passport CIS or a passport CIS operator violates any of applicable laws and regulations in the home or host economies.

ARFP = Asia Region Funds Passport, CIS = collective investment scheme.
Source: Asia-Pacific Economic Cooperation (APEC). https://fundspassport.apec.org.

---

[41] See https://fundspassport.apec.org.

Figure 15: Asia Region Funds Passport Collective Investment Scheme Authorization and Notification Process

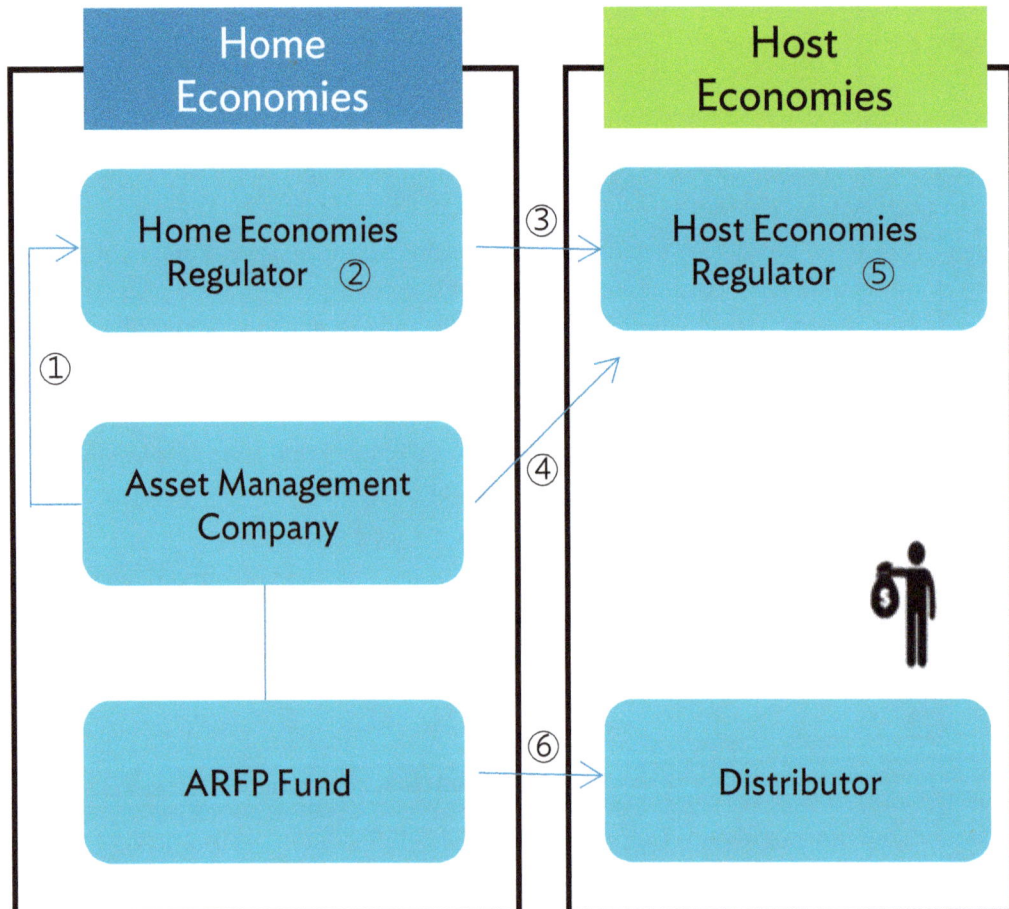

ARFP = Asia Region Funds Passport, CIS = collective investment scheme.

Notes:
- The CIS operator proven to be eligible in accordance with the ARFP rules should submit the application for registration to the home economy regulator.
- The application is reviewed by the home economy regulator. If approved, the regulator generates a designated code for the passport CIS.
- The regulator of the home economy notifies their counterpart in the host economy about the passport CIS registration.
- The CIS operator should provide the host economy regulator with the newly generated CIS code and required documents.
- The host economy regulator should review matters related to investor protection (e.g., distribution, disclosure) and register the passport CIS within 21 days.
- The CIS operator is able to initiate distribution in the host economy

Source: Asia-Pacific Economic Cooperation (APEC). https://fundspassport.apec.org.

The memorandum of cooperation of ARFP does not contain requirements on the settlement of subscription and redemption. The process for such settlement is well described in the Handbook on ARFP CIS Registration published by the Korea Financial Investment Association, as follows:

- The local agent in the home economy routes the order for subscription, redemption, or switching on behalf of the host economy distributor.
- The order is approved by the home economy CIS manager.
- The CIS manager sends a cash settlement instruction to the trustee.
- The cash settlement is executed between the host economy distributor and home economy trustee.
- The trustee (as for subscription) or the local agent (as for redemption) confirms the finality of cash settlement by changing the beneficial ownership in the account book of the host economy distributor.

Unlike the Central Securities Depository Regulation (CSDR) of Europe, there is no pan-Asian regulation that prescribes the settlement of cross-border transactions among Asian economies. Therefore, as for ARFP, the settlement between the host economy distributor and home economy trustee is likely to be carried out in a free-of-payment manner in the early phases.

Some policies in ARFP member economies may obscure settlement finality such as the "cooling-off rights" in Australia. The right to cool off allows an Australian investor to cancel a subscription or redemption order within 14 days after the order date and retrieve the cash or securities based on the valuation of the cool-off date.[42]

3.   *Statistics*

As of November 2021, there had been no transactions under ARFP. However, a Korean delegate of the ARFP Joint Committee has informed that a New Zealand asset management company has come close to launching the first ARFP CIS.

C.   **ASEAN Collective Investment Scheme**

1.   *Outline*

At the 13th ASEAN Summit in Singapore in November 2007, ASEAN leaders jointly adopted the ASEAN Economic Community Blueprint (AEC Blueprint) with the goal of establishing ASEAN as a single market and production base, with free flow of goods, services, investments, and skilled labor, and the freer flow of capital. The AEC Blueprint also sets out a general framework to strengthen ASEAN capital market development and integration.

---

[42]   Since the ARFP memorandum of cooperation states that the distribution of passport CIS is subject to host economy requirements, unique policies of each member economy, such as cooling-off rights, should be respected. It seems inevitable that cooling-off rights would undermine the finality of settlement.

On 1 October 2013, the ASEAN Capital Markets Forum (ACMF) announced that the Securities Commission Malaysia; the Monetary Authority of Singapore; and the Securities and Exchange Commission. Thailand had signed a memorandum of understanding to establish an ASEAN CIS framework for cross-border offerings of CIS (ASEAN CIS Framework). On 11 May 2021, the Securities and Exchange Commission of the Philippines became a signatory to ASEAN CIS.

The ASEAN CIS Framework allows the units of an ASEAN CIS authorized in its home jurisdiction to be offered in host jurisdictions under a streamlined authorization process, provided that the ASEAN CIS satisfies the set of common standards specified in the Standards of Qualifying CIS.[43]

2. *ASEAN Collective Investment Scheme: Standards of Qualifying Collective Investment Scheme*

The Standards of Qualifying CIS consist of two parts. The first part prescribes the qualifications of the CIS operator and trustee/fund supervisor/Independent Oversight Entity as demonstrated in Table 13, and the requirements relating to approval, valuation, and operational matters. The second part prescribes the product restrictions of qualifying CIS.

Table 13: ASEAN Collective Investment Scheme Home Regulator

Home Regulator	Entity That Can Conduct Independent Reviews
Malaysia	A chartered accountant who is registered with the Malaysian Institute of Accountants.
Singapore	A public accountant who is registered or deemed to be registered under the Accountants Act of Singapore or a trustee approved under the Securities and Futures Act.
Thailand	An auditor as defined by the Securities and Exchange Commission or the mutual fund supervisor appointed for the mutual fund under the Securities and Exchange Act, B.E. 2535.
Philippines	An independent accountant or auditor duly registered with the Board of Accountancy of the Professional Regulation Commission of the Philippines and accredited by the Securities and Exchange Commission.

ASEAN = Association of Southeast Asian Nations.
Source: Handbook for ASEAN CIS and Their Operators.

As part of the plan for the ASEAN Economic Community, ASEAN CIS has been designed with end goals and policy actions to accomplish periodic targets and milestones since 2016 (Table 14).

---

[43] ASEAN. 2021. *Handbook for ASEAN CIS and Their Operators.* Jakarta.

Table 14: ASEAN Economic Community 2025 Strategic Action Plans, 2016–2025

End Goal	Policy Action	2016–2017	2018–2019	2020–2021	2022–2025
			Target		
Facilitate cross-border CIS in ASEAN	Enhance market access for CIS under ASEAN CIS Framework	Provide clarity on issues raised by industry, including taxation and foreign exchange measures	Alignment of disclosure rules among signatory jurisdictions Address tax issues between locally domiciled CIS and passported CIS Address foreign exchange issues impeding implementation of the ASEAN CIS Framework At least 3 AMS are members of the ASEAN CIS Framework	Continued alignment of rules where discrepancies impede market access under ASEAN CIS Framework At least, 4 AMS are members of the ASEAN CIS Framework	Mutual recognition for economies under ASEAN CIS Framework At least 5 AMS are members of the ASEAN CIS Framework

End Goal	Policy Action	2016_2017	2018–2019	2020–2021	2022–2025
			Milestone		
		Issue FAQ to industry	Signatory jurisdictions to address tax issues between local and passported CIS Signatory jurisdictions to address foreign exchange issues impeding implementation of CIS Framework Signatory jurisdictions to work on the harmonization of disclosure rules Other AMS assess domestic regulatory requirements to join ASEAN CIS Framework	Other AMS assess domestic regulatory requirements to join ASEAN CIS Framework Signatory jurisdictions to continue work on common disclosure rules	Signatory jurisdictions to consider how to upgrade the ASEAN CIS Framework to support full mutual recognition Other AMS assess domestic regulatory requirements to join ASEAN CIS Framework

AMS = ASEAN member state, ASEAN = Association of Southeast Asian Nations, CIS= collective investment scheme, FAQ = frequently asked questions.

Notes: Only the CIS-related parts of the ASEAN Economic Community strategic action plans are described here. The ASEAN Framework for Cross-Border Offering of Collective Investment Schemes was operationalized in Malaysia, Singapore, and Thailand in August 2014.

Source: ASEAN Capital Markets Forum.

3. Statistics

The CIS registered under ASEAN CIS can be found at the official web page of ACMF (www.theacmf.org), which contains links directing to the relevant websites of Malaysia, Singapore, and Thailand (Tables 15 and 16).[44]

Table 15: Retail Schemes Approved as Qualifying Collective Investment Scheme under the ASEAN Collective Investment Scheme Framework of Singapore

No.	Outbound	Inbound (Home Jurisdiction)
1	Singapore Dividend Equity Fund	Principal ASEAN Dynamic Fund (Malaysia)
2	Schroder Asian Equity Yield Fund	Principal Malaysia Titans Plus Fund (Malaysia)
3	United Global Healthcare Fund	Principal Asia Pacific Dynamic Income Fund (Malaysia)

ASEAN = Association of Southeast Asian Nations.
Note: Information is as of the end of June 2020.
Source: Monetary Authority of Singapore. *Offers of Collective Investment Schemes.*

Table 16: List of Retail ASEAN Collective Investment Scheme for the General Public of Thailand

No.	Outbound	Date of Collective Investment Scheme Approval
1	Singapore Dividend Equity Fund	11 June 2015

ASEAN = Association of Southeast Asian Nations.
Note: All information is as of June 2020.
Source: Securities and Exchange Commission, Thailand. https://www.sec.or.th/en/Pages/LawandRegulations/ASEANCollectiveInvestmentSchemes.aspx#list.

D. Mutual Recognition of Funds

The Mutual Recognition of Funds (MRF) differs from multilateral passport schemes since it involves only two economies, albeit both are pursuing the harmonization and standardization of CIS registration just like CIS passports. Since the early 2000s, Asia and the Pacific has abounded with MRFs: the Australia–New Zealand MRF in June 2008; Hong Kong, China–Australia MRF in July 2008; the People's Republic of China (PRC)–Hong Kong, China MRF in July 2015; and Hong Kong, China–Thailand MRF in January 2021.[45]

In particular, the Hong Kong Monetary Authority (HKMA) has made serious efforts to initiate its MRF with the PRC, such as by launching the dedicated platform CMU Fund Order Routing and Settlement Service (FORS) in 2009.

---

[44] The official website of the Securities Commission Malaysia contains CIS statistics in general and does not offer ASEAN CIS-specific data visibility. Please refer to https://www.sc.com.my/analytics/fund-management-products%20.

[45] The Hong Kong, China–Thailand MRF came into effect on 16 June 2021 after the Securities and Futures Commission of Hong Kong (SFC) and the SEC entered into a Memorandum of Understanding on the Mutual Recognition of Funds on 20 January 2021 to allow eligible public CIS in Hong Kong, China and Thailand to be distributed in each other's markets through a streamlined process. Please refer to the SFC's press release dated 20 January 2021.

As a gateway for accessing investment opportunities in the PRC, the MRF is one of the best examples demonstrating the PRC's drive for market liberalization.

On 22 May 2015, the Securities and Futures Commission of Hong Kong (SFC) and the China Securities Regulatory Commission (CSRC) signed the Memorandum of Regulatory Cooperation on PRC–Hong Kong Mutual Recognition of Funds.

This memorandum allows eligible PRC CIS and Hong Kong, China CIS to be distributed in each other's markets through a streamlined vetting process. The scheme was to be implemented on 1 July 2015. At launch, the initial quota for the MRF was set at CNY300 billion for inflows and outflows of CIS in each direction, and there is no requirement for quota application as utilization is on a first-come, first-served basis.

Table 17 describes the eligible CIS for MRF as of 2020.

Table 17: Eligibility of Mutual Recognition of Funds Collective Investment Scheme

Establishment Requirement	• Established, managed, and operated in accordance with the laws and regulations of home economy jurisdiction
	• Regulated by the regulatory body in the home economy jurisdiction
	• Publicly offered CIS domiciled in the home economy jurisdiction
	• Managed and operated for +1 year since establishment
Minimum CIS Size	• Not less than CNY200 million (or its equivalent in a different currency)
Scope of Investment	• Not primarily invested in the host economy market
	• Equity CIS, mixed CIS, bond CIS, unlisted index CIS, and physical index-tracking exchange traded CIS
Value of Sales	• Value of shares or units in the CIS sold to investors in the host economy jurisdiction shall not be more than 50% of the value of the CIS' total assets
Representative	• Must appoint a licensed or registered firm in the host jurisdiction to be its representative.

CIS = collective investment scheme, CNY = Chinese yuan.

Source: Bank of China (Hong Kong). Mutual Recognition of Funds (MRF) Education Corner. www.bochk.com/en/investment/fund/step1/mrf.html.

The HKMA has established an automated and standardized STP platform in cooperation with the China Securities Depository and Clearing Corporation (CSDC), Shenzhen Stock Exchange (SZSE), and Shenzhen Securities Communication Co. Ltd. (SSCC), supporting the following functions:[46]

▶ Routing order instructions among distributors, transfer agents, and fund houses with regard subscription and redemption;

▶ Sending and receiving cash settlement instructions for subscription and redemption;

---

[46]   CSDC, or ChinaClear, is known to provide transfer agent services for open-end CIS in the PRC. The SSCC is the communications server provider owned by SZSE (majority shareholders), ChinaClear, and the China Academy of Space Technology.

- Sending and receiving MRF-related investment information (net asset value [NAV], corporate action schedules, CIS status);
- Sending and receiving operational information of trustees; and
- Periodic reporting on other CIS.

For the effective execution of the aforementioned tasks, the PRC and Hong Kong, China have defined their respective roles and responsibilities as outlined below:

- The SSCC operates the Financial Data Exchange Platform (FDEP), which features various functions—including information sharing, the exchange of order instructions, and the distribution of reports—among the CIS players in the PRC. The SSCC serves as an STP platform for MRF.
- ChinaClear is connected with FDEP to serve as a transfer agent for the PRC CIS and also the sub-transfer agent for Hong Kong, China CIS. As for southbound transaction, despite having the record of retail investor orders, ChinaClear routes orders to transfer agents or fund houses in Hong Kong, China under the nominee accounts of Chinese distributors. When it comes to northbound transaction, Hong Kong, China distributors directly open accounts at ChinaClear, which then serves as the transfer agent for Hong Kong Funds.
- The Central Moneymarkets Unit (CMU) of HKMA links with FDEP to assist with Hong Kong, China distributors, asset managers, and transfer agents to carry out operational engagement with their Chinese counterparties.

The order and settlement for MRF is designed as seen in Figure 16.

Even if the MRF scheme has allowed for much flexibility, such as the PRC's adoption of nominee account structure, the scheme is not without limitations, as follows (Figure 17):[47]

- **Quota restriction.** MRF transaction is confined to an investment quota, hence, leaving room for the possibility that a subscription order may be declined when the quota is maxed out.
- **Strict eligibility.** There is a possibility that additional subscription can be declined. For instance, if the PRC CIS does not continue to meet its MRF eligibility requirements, Hong Kong, China investors are no longer allowed to apply for additional subscription. The strictness of eligibility should be taken into consideration in terms of investment sustainability.
- **Tax uncertainty.** The Chinese tax authorities still have not clarified taxations for the northbound investments via the MRF scheme, inevitably exposing the PRC investors to unexpected costs depending on any policy changes in the future.
- **Gaps in market practices.** Market practices in the PRC and Hong Kong, China may be different. In addition, the operational arrangements of recognized PRC CIS and other public CIS offered in Hong Kong, China may be different in certain ways. For example, a recognized PRC CIS may only accept subscriptions or redemption of units on a day when both the PRC and Hong Kong, China markets are open, or it may have different cut-off times or dealing day arrangements versus other Hong Kong, China CIS.

---

47 Bank of China (Hong Kong). No date. Mutual Recognition of Funds Education Corner. Hong Kong, China.

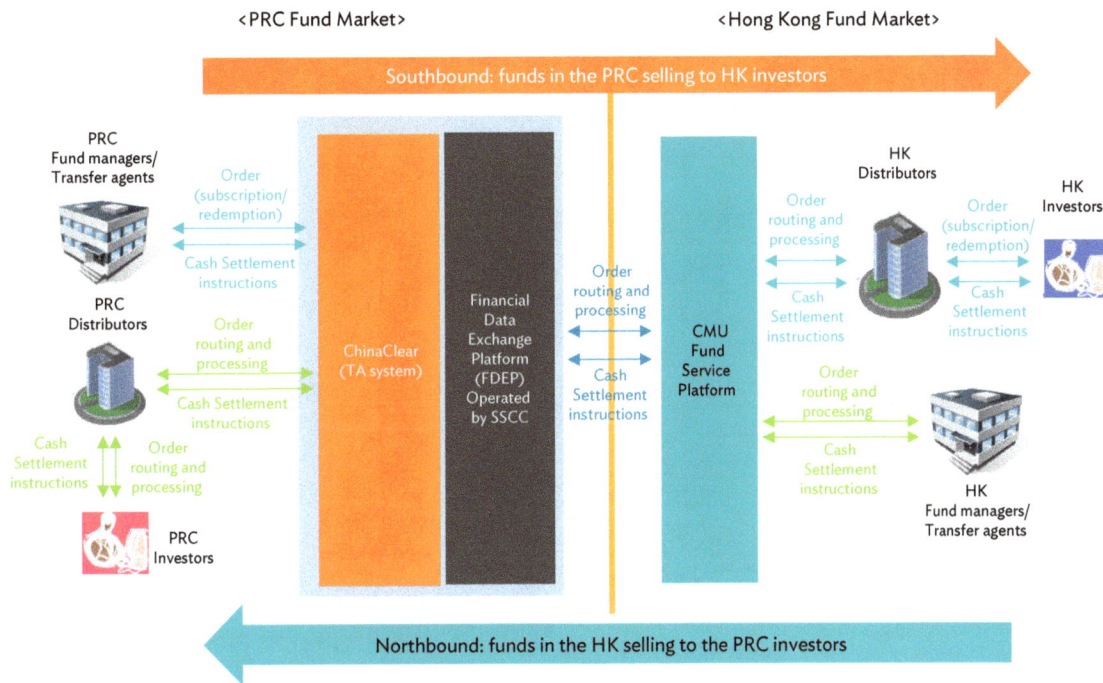

Figure 16: Order and Settlement of Mutual Recognition of Funds

CMU = Central Moneymarkets Unit; HK = Hong Kong, China; PRC = People's Republic of China; SSCC = Shenzhen Securities Communication Co. Ltd.; TA = transfer agent.

Source: Illustration by the Hong Kong Monetary Authority.

▶ **CNY currency and conversion risks.** The Chinese yuan is currently not freely convertible and is subject to exchange controls and restrictions. Non-CNY-based investors are exposed to foreign exchange risks and there is no guarantee that the value of the Chinese yuan against the investors' base currencies (for example, the Hong Kong dollar) will not depreciate.

▶ **Others.** CIS primarily investing in securities related to the PRC market may be subject to additional concentration risks. Compared to investment in other markets, investing in the PRC can give rise to different risks including political, policy, tax, economic, foreign exchange, legal, regulatory, and liquidity risks.

Figure 17: Number of Mutual Recognition of Funds in the People's Republic of China and Hong Kong, China

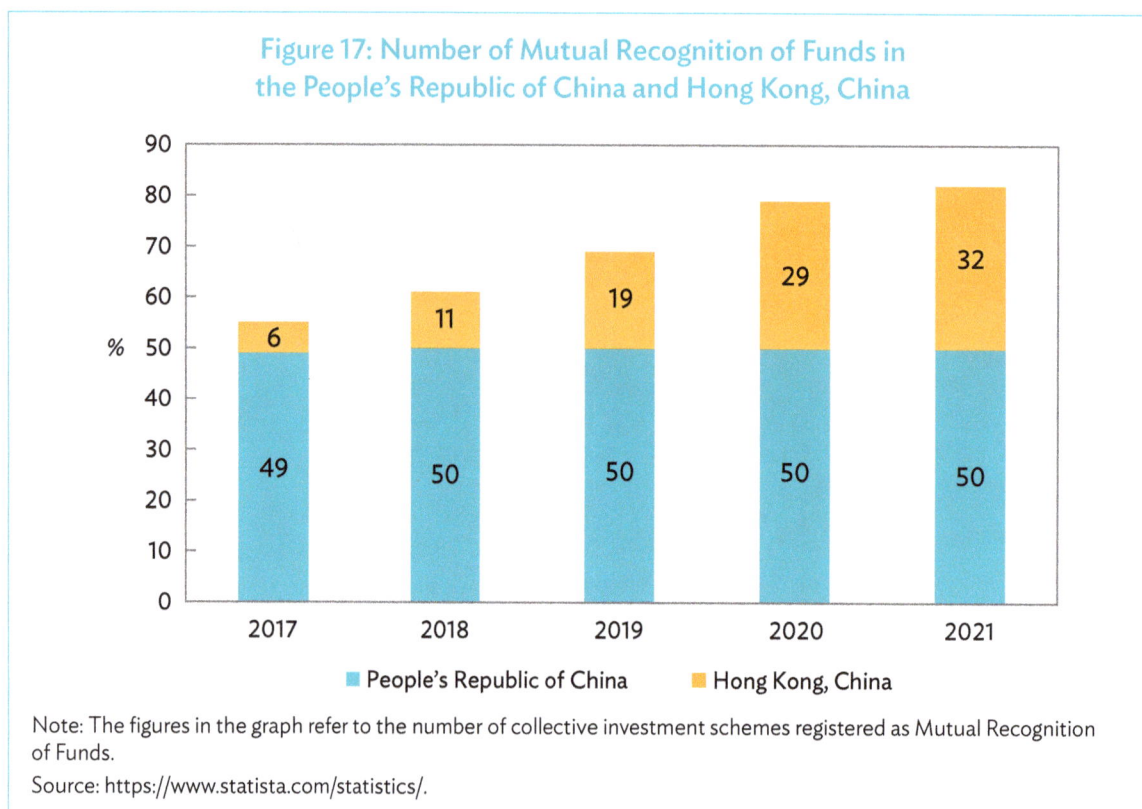

Note: The figures in the graph refer to the number of collective investment schemes registered as Mutual Recognition of Funds.

Source: https://www.statista.com/statistics/.

E. Implications

1. *Collective Investment Scheme Industry Gaps among ASEAN+3 Economies*

The CIS market landscape of ASEAN+3 is a mixture of a few highly advanced economies with massive transaction volume and global marketability (e.g., Hong Kong, China; Japan; and Singapore) and followers that need more time to build a solid CIS market. Such quantitative and qualitative market gaps should be taken into account when discussing regional standardization.

2. *Necessity of Tailored Approach*

More than half of the ASEAN+3 economies (the PRC, Japan, the Republic of Korea, Malaysia, the Philippines, Singapore, and Thailand) are engaging in either bilateral or multilateral regulatory frameworks for cross-border transaction whereas the rest have no plans for importing and exporting CIS. Even among those participating in passport schemes or MRF, the scale of inbound and outbound transaction varies drastically. Therefore, as evidenced by Europe's success with UCITS, a targeted-and-staged approach is required when applying the central securities depository and real-time gross settlement (CSD-RTGS) linkage model as a pan-Asian settlement system for regional CIS transaction.

3. *Promotion of Platform-Based Processing*

It was found in the survey that five economies use CSD-run central platforms while two economies have private platforms. These economies seem to use STP platforms to process the subscription and redemption of CIS. In particular, the platforms of Hong Kong, China; the Republic of Korea; and Thailand are connected with those of ICSDs and use International Organization for Standardization (ISO)-compliant messages for transaction-related communication.[48]

A good case in point is the multiple communication channels of the HKMA's CMU FORS. CMU FORS allows its participants to send and receive messages in the format of their preference. For instance, CMU FORS can translate the counterparty's ISO-compliant message into local proprietary messages upon the request of participants. Such best practice can be a rich source of inspiration for other ASEAN+3 economies seeking an STP benchmark.

4. *Drive for Delivery versus Payment*

The research found that only three economies (Indonesia, Japan, and the Republic of Korea) perform DVP settlements via central securities depository Securities Settlement System (CSD SSS)–central bank processing standardization linkage, while other economies process CIS settlements separately in a cash leg and a securities leg. As of 2020, the regulatory bodies participating in ARFP and ASEAN CIS appeared to be not yet focused on the necessity of establishing a DVP settlement system for cross-border transaction of CIS.

Also, it was found in the survey that most of the respondent economies have pertinent laws and regulations to ensure settlement completeness, while some economies seem to have no legal safeguards for settlement finality.

All things considered, it may take some time to apply DVP as a settlement standard for the CIS traded among ASEAN+3 economies given regulatory hurdles, lacking infrastructure, and differing market maturity in the ASEAN+3 region. However, as in the case of UCITS, DVP settlement standardization is an inevitable destination if ASEAN+3 aspires to make its CIS passport schemes free from risks and more efficient and globally marketable. In this sense, more interdisciplinary research is needed to explore the feasibility of applying the CSD RTGS model to CIS cross-border transactions.

---

[48] The author assumes that Japan and Singapore also have linked up via ICSDs for cross-border transactions.

V. RECOMMENDATIONS ON THE APPLICATION OF THE CSD-RTGS LINKAGE MODEL TO ASIAN COLLECTIVE INVESTMENT SCHEME PASSPORTS

The collective investment scheme (CIS) is an indirect portfolio investment undertaken by a professional manager for the purpose of stable and profitable management. Many economies attempt to familiarize their growing elderly populations with CIS as an effective means of post-retirement wealth management and provide policy and legal support to ensure that CIS can serve as a long-term investing vehicle on the demand side of their local securities market.

In the case of Europe, the Undertaking for Collective Investment in Transferable Securities (UCITS) was launched to achieve economies of scale in the regional CIS industry. Under the vision of creating a single regional market, what Europe promoted to make UCITS more efficient included the standardization of order routing processing and the implementation of delivery versus payment (DVP) settlement based on the premise that post-trade harmonization and a viable DVP settlement environment were the prerequisite for streamlining the regional CIS passport scheme.

Asia currently has two multilateral CIS passport schemes (the Asia Region Funds Passport [ARFP] and the ASEAN CIS) and multiple Mutual Recognition of Funds (MRFs) in order to bolster the global competitiveness of the regional CIS industry and ultimately channel Asian savings to regional investments. Given the latest developments of passport CIS, however, such ambition seems to be a remote prospect for now.

Based on the lessons learned from UCITS, this study offers recommendations as follows for enhancing the efficiency of Asian bond and passport CIS markets.

A. Recommendation 1: Look Beyond Bonds and More Broadly Apply the CSD-RTGS Linkage Model to Collective Investment Scheme Passports in Asia

This report suggests applying the central securities depository and real-time gross settlement (CSD-RTGS) DVP linkage to both bonds and CIS as a regional integrated settlement engine. This report also includes the rationale for and developments surrounding Europe's implementation of the DVP settlement of UCITS CIS. In the case of UCITS, the inefficiencies of cross-border securities trading have been largely reduced via the standardization of order routing and settlement processes and the implementation of TARGET2-Securities (T2S)—the pan-European DVP engine that connects regional CSDs and central banks. In fact, T2S is not just confined to CIS trading but also settles the cross-border transactions of equities, bonds, and many other securities within Europe. In this way, Europe has maximized the post-trade efficiency of securities industry under an integrated settlement engine.

The European model of a single integrated system managed by a single responsible entity may not be a cure-all for the Asian post-trade conundrum since capital markets differ by region. However, there are still lessons to be learned to ensure more efficient intra-regional, cross-border trading in Asia. Like what Europe has achieved under UCITS, Asia can greatly reduce inefficiencies via the standardization of post-trade practices and implementation of DVP settlement. For this, it is not necessary to enact new laws or introduce a single currency for the region. Rather, such a goal can be accomplished by broadly applying the CSD-RTGS model proposed by the Cross-Border Settlement Infrastructure Forum (CSIF) in the Asian context.

Unlike the initial concept, the CSD-RTGS linkage harbors ample potential as a DVP engine that settles the cross-border transactions of passport CIS, not just bonds. Therefore, if the cross-border transactions of CIS, as well as bonds, become eligible for settlement on a CSD-RTGS linkage platform, it will lay a solid foundation for the post-trade standardization of the Asian capital markets in the long term (Figure 18).

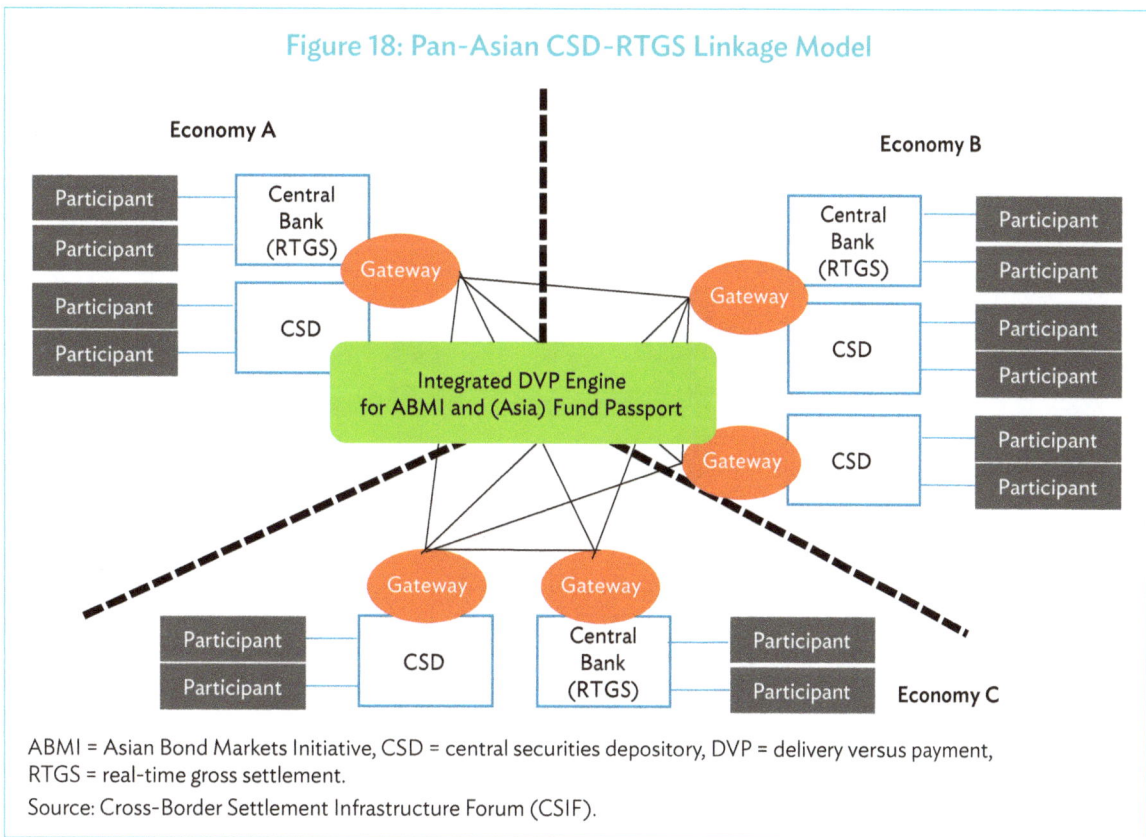

Figure 18: Pan-Asian CSD-RTGS Linkage Model

ABMI = Asian Bond Markets Initiative, CSD = central securities depository, DVP = delivery versus payment, RTGS = real-time gross settlement.
Source: Cross-Border Settlement Infrastructure Forum (CSIF).

B. Recommendation 2: Connect the Asian Bond Markets Initiative, Passport Schemes, and Other Relevant Post-Trade Groups to Form a "Back-to-Front" Cooperation Framework in the Asian Collective Investment Scheme Industry under the Leadership of the Cross-Border Settlement Infrastructure Forum

A group of diverse stakeholders are required to set in motion a grand plan. For the success of UCITS, the European Commission clarified basic directions and strategies in the white paper on *Enhancing the Single Market Framework for Investment Funds*. For the CIS sector, the European Fund and Asset Management Association (EFAMA) took the initiative to establish industry standards. European central banks made concerted efforts to develop and launch T2S in linkage with regional CSDs to execute DVP settlements.

In this sense, Asia also needs to create an interdisciplinary cooperation framework, as demonstrated in Figure 19, which facilitates regional dialogue among the relevant bodies in the front-office and back-office sectors of the securities industry. In pursuit of post-trade harmonization, CSIF should lead such a framework to consult with policy makers and industry players to produce recommendations and standards.

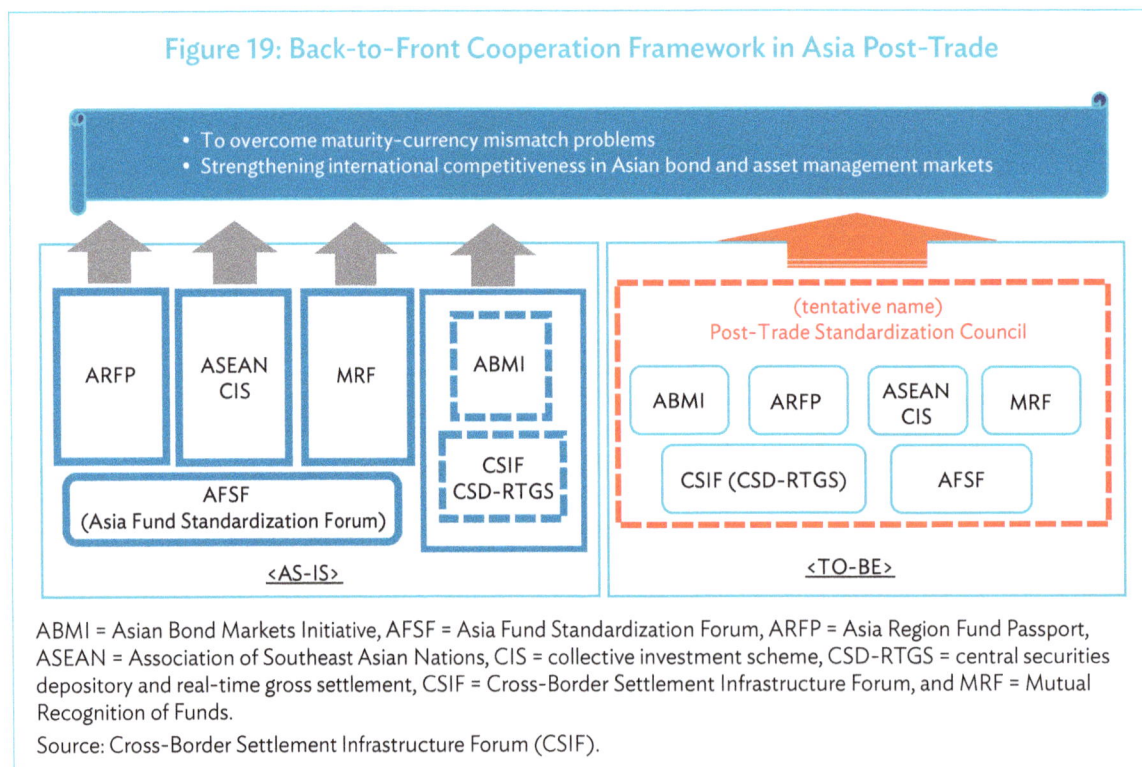

Figure 19: Back-to-Front Cooperation Framework in Asia Post-Trade

ABMI = Asian Bond Markets Initiative, AFSF = Asia Fund Standardization Forum, ARFP = Asia Region Fund Passport, ASEAN = Association of Southeast Asian Nations, CIS = collective investment scheme, CSD-RTGS = central securities depository and real-time gross settlement, CSIF = Cross-Border Settlement Infrastructure Forum, and MRF = Mutual Recognition of Funds.
Source: Cross-Border Settlement Infrastructure Forum (CSIF).

The aforementioned cooperation framework should ensure the following:

▶ The CIS settlement of ARFP and ASEAN CIS is executed on a DVP basis, for which the common rules of the passport schemes should be amended.

▶ CSIF consults with the Asia Fund Standardization Forum (AFSF) to expedite the adoption of the CSD-RTGS linkage as a standard model for CIS settlement (Figure 20).[49]

Figure 20: Overview of Asia Fund Standardization Forum

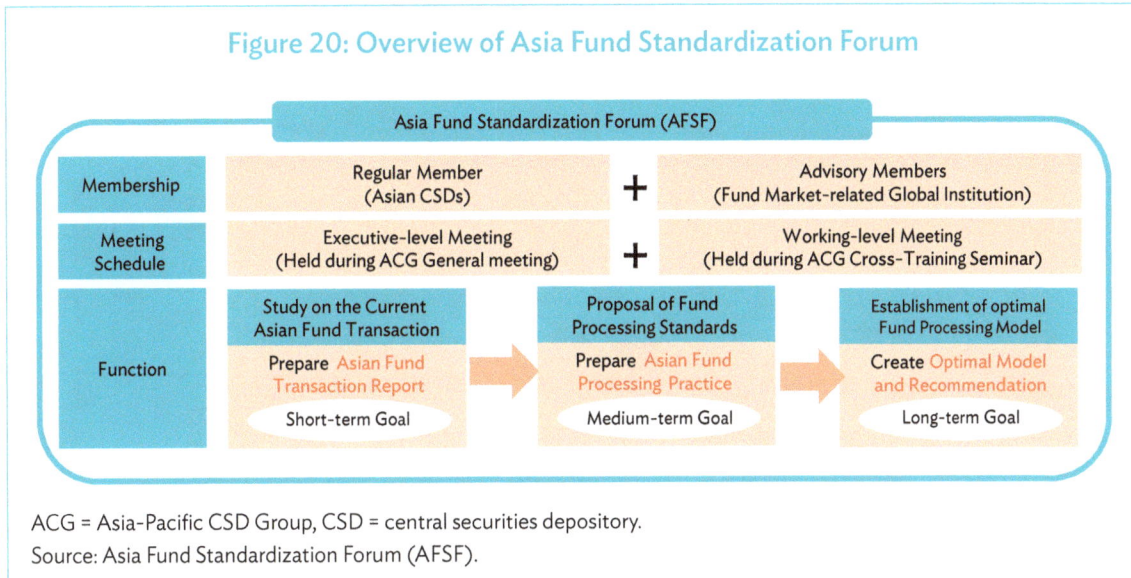

Asia Fund Standardization Forum (AFSF)

Membership	Regular Member (Asian CSDs)	**+**	Advisory Members (Fund Market-related Global Institution)
Meeting Schedule	Executive-level Meeting (Held during ACG General meeting)	**+**	Working-level Meeting (Held during ACG Cross-Training Seminar)

Function

Study on the Current Asian Fund Transaction	→	Proposal of Fund Processing Standards	→	Establishment of optimal Fund Processing Model
Prepare Asian Fund Transaction Report		**Prepare** Asian Fund Processing Practice		**Create** Optimal Model and Recommendation
Short-term Goal		Medium-term Goal		Long-term Goal

ACG = Asia-Pacific CSD Group, CSD = central securities depository.
Source: Asia Fund Standardization Forum (AFSF).

C.   Recommendation 3: Secure the Finality of Delivery versus Payment Settlement Based on Sound Legal Grounds

One of the most crucial elements of a DVP model is the finality of settlement, which is mostly ensured by establishing solid legal grounds.

In the case of Europe, the finality of settlement is legally mandated by Central Securities Depository Regulation (CSDR) and the Directive 98/26/EC of the European Parliament and of the Council on Settlement Finality in Payment and Securities Settlement Systems. The regulations govern not only domestic trading but also cross-border financial instruments like passport CIS and make sure the finality of settlement stands firm and uncompromising, even in the event of counterparty insolvency.

Such regulatory foundation must be built if Asia aspires to establish CSD-RTGS linkage as an integrated DVP settlement model for bond and CIS transactions in the region.

---

[49] Since its inception in 2015 at the 19th General Meeting of Asia-Pacific CSD Group, the AFSF has long facilitated regional dialogue on the post-trade harmonization of CIS transactions with the ultimate aim to build the most ideal post-trade processing model for cross-border CIS trading in Asia.

For this, the laws and regulations on the general aspects of DVP settlement need to be revisited, such as the DVP eligibility of members and instruments, registration of settlement instructions, execution of settlement obligations, simultaneous settlement requirements, and roles of CSDs and central banks.

CSIF can refer to the case of ARFP in this regard. ARFP members drafted and agreed on common passport rules, reflected the rules and the relevant obligations into the memorandum of cooperation, and transposed the memorandum of cooperation's requirements into the laws and sub-regulations of each member jurisdiction under the approval of the local authorities.

D. Recommendation 4: Explore Ways to Enhance the Efficiency of the CSD-RTGS Delivery versus Payment Engine for Asian Bond and Passport CIS Trading

Firstly, it is strongly recommended to consider CIS central platforms or order routing systems as gateways for a CSD-RTGS linkage system.

CSIF defines the key functions of the CSD-RTGS gateways as "network connection" and "message conversion" (Figure 21).

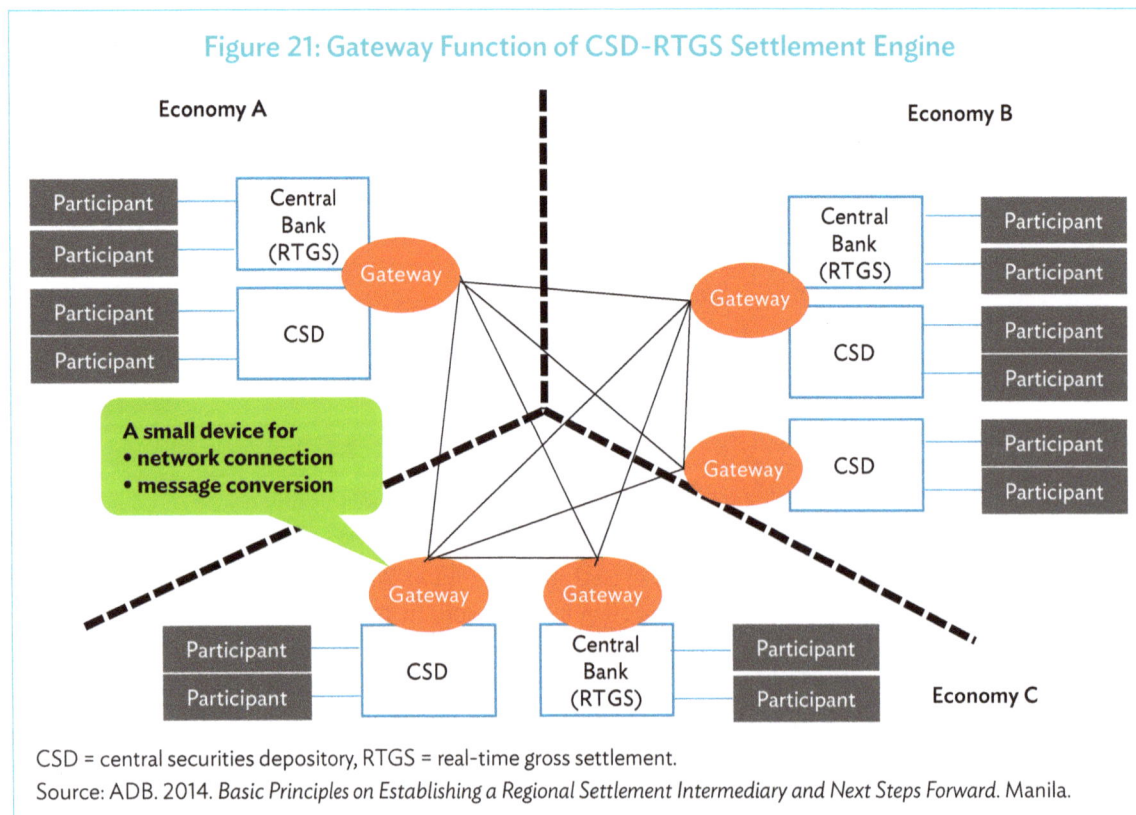

Figure 21: Gateway Function of CSD-RTGS Settlement Engine

CSD = central securities depository, RTGS = real-time gross settlement.
Source: ADB. 2014. *Basic Principles on Establishing a Regional Settlement Intermediary and Next Steps Forward*. Manila.

The two rounds of CSIF surveys found that many Asian economies have built CIS order-routing systems in linkage with settlement systems. In particular, the order-routing systems of Hong Kong, China; Thailand; Japan; and the Republic of Korea are able to connect networks and convert messages as gateways for both domestic CIS and UCITS CIS. Such findings will yield invaluable insights for CSIF to develop the aforementioned gateways and implement an integrated settlement engine for both bond and CIS transactions. Settlement system integration can be achieved if the messaging formats for settling bond transactions are developed and embedded into regional order routing platforms, which exchange mutually agreed or ISO-compliant messages.

In addition, CSIF needs to study the netting effects on cash settlement if Asian bond and passport CIS transactions are settled by an integrated DVP system. The CSD-RTGS model proposed by CSIF operates via bilateral linkage on a transaction-by-transaction basis. The model may be the best fit for bonds since the number of transactions is relatively small.

However, if the CSD-RTGS model embraces CIS transactions, it may become possible to take advantage of netting effects via centralized settlement that is executed at a fixed time, although such a method is a matter of negotiation among settlement parties depending on the advancement of settlement.

Appendix

OVERVIEW OF ASEAN+3 COLLECTIVE INVESTMENT SCHEME MARKETS

This appendix is derived from the two rounds of Cross-Border Settlement Infrastructure Forum (CSIF) survey involving Association of Southeast Asian Nations plus the People's Republic of China, Japan, and the Republic of Korea (ASEAN+3) members. Analyzed to draw out insights for this report if necessary, the survey responses are attached as appendix without extra editing. Although most of the members faithfully participated in the survey, some were not able to fully answer the survey questionnaire. For more solid information sourcing, the CSIF consultant took reference from the reports of Asia Fund Standardization Forum (AFSF) and the publications of central securities depositories (CSDs), central banks, and state regulators.

A. Brunei Darussalam

1. Market Size of Collective Investment Scheme

A collective investment scheme (CIS) is regulated under the Securities Markets Order, 2013 (SMO).

Section 203 of SMO defines CIS any investment arrangements with respect to assets of any description, including money, the purpose or effect of which is to enable persons taking part in the arrangements (whether by becoming owners of the property or any part of it or otherwise) to participate in or receive profits or income arising from the acquisition, holding, management, or disposal of the property or sums paid out of such profits or income with the following details:

▶ The Monetary Authority of Brunei Darussalam (AMBD) approves CIS, which are offered to retail and non-retail investors by granting a CIS license or via recognition.[1] The CIS can be offered either to the public or via private placement. Those wishing to operate or manage a CIS will need to apply for a CIS license from AMBD.

▶ The application must be made to AMBD by the operator and custodian, or proposed operator or custodian, of the CIS (Section 209, SMO). The licensed CIS is required to comply with the requirements as set out in the SMO and the Securities Market Regulations (SMR).

▶ A foreign CIS to be offered in Brunei Darussalam will need to apply for recognition. Recognition may be granted where the economy or territory to which the foreign CIS is managed and licensed in is designated by the AMBD.

---

[1] The Autoriti Monetari Brunei Darussalam (AMBD) refers to the Monetary Authority of Brunei Darussalam.

A CIS may be classified as a private CIS if it fulfills certain conditions, as follows:

▶ Units in the CIS are only offered for sale or issuance with specific classes of investors. The list of specific classes of investors can be found under Section 20, SMO.

▶ Units are offered in a manner that does not result in the CIS having more than 50 unitholders (Regulation 185, SMR).

▶ In Brunei Darussalam, there is no home-domiciled CIS yet while offshore CIS are imported via inbound transaction channels.

Table A1.1: Inbound Transaction of Collective Investment Scheme in Brunei Darussalam

Saudi Arabia	Singapore	Luxembourg	Ireland	Malaysia	SUM
4	9	6	1	2	22

Note: Information is as of the end of 2020.
Source: ADB Cross-Border Settlement Infrastructure Forum (CSIF) Survey.

2.   *Legal Structure of CIS*

Collective Investment Scheme Type	Open-End vs. Closed-End	Redeemable vs. Traded on Exchange	Investment Company vs. Unincorporated	Market Share (%)
Unit trust	Open-end	Redeemable	Unincorporated	68
Investment company	Open-end	Redeemable	Investment company	31

Note: Information is as of the end of 2020.
Source: ADB Cross-Border Settlement Infrastructure Forum (CSIF) Survey.

3.   *Distribution Channel*

Distribution Channel (%)				Electronic Platform Available?
Bank	Securities Company	Insurance Company	Others	
100				

Note: Information is as of the end of 2020.
Source: ADB Cross-Border Settlement Infrastructure Forum (CSIF) Survey.

4.   *Issuance of Collective Investment Scheme Unit*

Service Coverage	Description
X	CIS units are issued in the form of physical certificate, contract note, and confirmation advice, which are mailed out to investors and clients. CIS units are not required to be deposited at CSD.

CIS = collective investment scheme, CSD = central securities depository.
Note: Information is as of the end of 2020.
Source: ADB Cross-Border Settlement Infrastructure Forum (CSIF) Survey.

5. Cross-Border Collective Investment Scheme Distribution

Home-Domiciled Collective Investment Scheme Sold Abroad (Outbound) Yes or No?	Foreign Collective Investment Schemes Sold in Your Economy (Inbound)		
	Yes or No	Data	Pertinent Laws
No	Yes	24	• Securities Markets Order, 2013 • Securities Markets Regulations, 2015

Note: Information is as of the end of 2020.
Source: ADB Cross-Border Settlement Infrastructure Forum (CSIF) Survey.

6. Central Platforms in Brunei Darussalam

In Brunei Darussalam, it is not mandated by law to establish clearing platforms and there is no linkage with an international central securities depository (ICSD) platform.

7. Collective Investment Scheme Settlement Model and Completeness and Finality of Settlement

Settlement of Subscription and Redemption
Brunei Darussalam has no requirement for CIS units to be subscribed or redeemed on the CSD level. Instead, CIS subscription and redemption are individually processed by distributors based on their internal processes and procedures.

In general, the workflow of CIS processing is similar among all licensed distributors in Brunei Darussalam. Subscribed units are remitted from a client's account (savings or current account) to the client's trading account (in one case, a trading account is not required) to the distributor's "temporary" account, which may be in the form of a transitory, trust, or settlement account.

Upon further confirmation of the client's subscription order by the administrator, the CIS units will then be remitted from the "temporary" account to the respective CIS administrator (if appointed) and finally to the respective CIS provider. As for redemption, the operational flow moves in the opposite direction.

Requirements on Issuance and Redemption of Public Collective Investment Scheme Units
The 2015 (SMR) Regulation 98 of the SMR prescribes the requirements on the issuance and redemption of public CIS. The essential parts of the regulation are extracted and presented in Box A1.1.

Legal Requirements on Settlement Finality
Currently, Brunei Darussalam has no regulations or requirements in place on the cancellation or nullification of an already-settled trade.

> ### Box A1.1: Selected 2015 (SMR) Regulation 98 of the SMR
>
> 98. (1) An operator of a public collective investment scheme must, at all times during the dealing day, be willing to issue and effect the sale of units in the public collective investment scheme to any eligible client in accordance with any conditions in the constitution and the prospectus, which must be fair and reasonable as between all unit holders and prospective unit holders for whom the operator does not have reasonable grounds to refuse such sale.
>
> (2) An operator of a public collective investment scheme must, at all times during the dealing day, effect redemption of units owned by a prospective unit holder, on the request of that prospective unit holder in accordance with any conditions in the constitution and the prospectus, unless the operator has reasonable grounds to refuse such redemption.
>
> (3) On agreeing to the redemption of units under sub-regulation (2), the operator must pay the full proceeds of the redemption to the unit holder within any reasonable period specified in the constitution or the prospectus unless it has reasonable grounds for withholding the payment.
>
> (4) The operator of the public collective investment scheme must make payment of proceeds on redemption in any manner provided for in the prospectus that must be fair and reasonable as between redeeming unit holders and continuing unit holders.
>
> (5) If a public collective investment scheme is a closed-ended public collective investment scheme, the operator must have in place arrangements to ensure that the issue, sale, and redemption of units of the public collective investment scheme are consistent with the closed-ended nature of the public collective investment scheme. The operator may also make provision for the issue of units of the public collective investment scheme through private placement provided those provisions are not inconsistent with the closed-ended nature of the public collective investment scheme.
>
> Source: ADB Cross-Border Settlement Infrastructure Forum (CSIF) Survey.

B.   People's Republic of China

1.   *Market Size of Collective Investment Scheme*

AUM (A)	GDP (G)	A/G (%)	No. of CIS	Note
USD5.659 trillion	USD15.504 trillion	36.5	107,731	

AUM = assets under management, CIS = collective investment scheme, GDP = gross domestic product.
Note: Information is as of the end of 2020.
Source: Asia Fund Standardization Forum Survey.

2.   *Legal Structure of Collective Investment Scheme*

Collective Investment Scheme Type	Open-end vs. Closed-end	Redeemable vs. Traded on Exchange	Investment Company vs. Unincorporated	Market Share (%)
Unit Trust				100

Note: Information is as of the end of 2020.
Source: Asia Fund Standardization Forum Survey.

3.   *Distribution Channel*

Fund Company	Bank	Independent Fund Sales Agency	Securities Company	Others
USD1.75 trillion (57.29%)	USD719 billion (23.59%)	USD336 billion (11.03%)	USD231 billion (5.79%)	USD15 billion (0.49%)

USD = United States dollar.
Note: Information is as of the end of 2020.
Source: Asia Fund Standardization Forum Survey.

4.   *Cross-Border Collective Investment Scheme Distribution*

Home-Domiciled Collective Investment Scheme Sold Abroad (Outbound) Yes or No?	Foreign Collective Investment Schemes Sold in Your Economy (Inbound)	
	Yes or No	Data
USD8.26 billion	Yes	• 27 (the number of Mutual Recognition of Funds) • USD2.64 billion

USD = United States dollar.
Note: Information is as of the end of 2020.
Source: Asia Fund Standardization Forum Survey.

5.   *Central Platforms in the People's Republic of China*

The communication system of the China Securities Depository and Clearing Corporation's (CSDC) CIS system is on a single-point connection mode to centrally connect participants, thereby greatly reducing contacts among and operational costs of participants.[2] According to the deployment of the China Securities Regulatory Commission (CSRC), CSDC launched the Central Data Exchange Platform (CDEP) at the end of September 2011. By the end of 2012, all transfer agents and CIS distributors gained complete access to the CDEP.

The CDEP is a transfer agent model. After processing, the results are sent to the CDEP for data backup.

C.   Cambodia

1.   *CIS Settlement Model and Completeness and Finality of Settlement*

Settlement of Subscription and Redemption

If CIS units are deposited at the Cambodia Securities Exchange (CSX), the CSX is responsible for the settlement of subscription and redemption. Since DVP3 is adopted in Cambodia, it is banks that perform cash settlement in the national bank system.[3] Every CIS unit is electronically recorded and not issued

---

[2]   The CSDC is also known as ChinaClear.
[3]   DvP model 3 typically settles both securities and funds on a net basis, with final transfers of both securities and funds occurring at the end of the processing cycle. (Taken from the BIS Glossary.)

in the form of physical certificate. If a unitholder needs a balance statement, he or she can request one from the CSD through his/her broker right after the unit is deposited in his/her balance.

Settlement Requirements

In Cambodia, when a CIS unit is traded and deposited at the CSX, it is settled in the same way as stocks or bonds and recorded under securities firms' account in the sub-account of investors.

Settlement Finality

Although unsettled trades can be canceled under the CSX Trading Rule, the trades that are already settled cannot be canceled.

According to the CSX Guideline on trade correction, if confused about a trade order (e.g., mistakenly exceeding the requested number of shares), broker may request to CSX (before noon time of T+1) to migrate the exceeded number of shares for broker to settle it (settlement date on T+2).

Box A1.2: Cambodia Securities Exchange Clearing and Settlement Operating Rule

Article 10. Procedures for Clearing and Settlement Operations

The Operator of Securities Clearing and Settlement Facility of the Cambodia Securities Exchange (CSX) shall calculate the quantity of securities and the amount of cash to be settled by member or participant by netting the securities and cash of each member or participants to be settled in the same day.

The Operator of Securities Clearing and Settlement Facility of the CSX shall notify the following matters to the members or participants on the clearing and settlement dates:

(1)   The dates of clearing and settlement,

(2)   The quantity and type of each securities to be settled by members or participants or on behalf of their clients, and

(3)   The amount of cash to be settled by members or participants or on behalf of their clients.

The quantity of securities and the amount of cash to be settled shall be calculated by the following methods:

(1)   **In case of securities:** obtained by clearing the total sold quantity and total purchased quantity per issue for the concerned member or participant,

(2)   **In case of cash:** obtained by clearing the total purchased value and the total sold value of concerned member or participants.

The member or participant shall transfer the securities and cash subject to settlement to the accounts of the Operator of Securities Clearing and Settlement Facility of the CSX before 8:30 AM on the settlement date and the Operator of a Securities Clearing and Settlement Facility of the CSX shall transfer those securities and cash to the beneficial members or participants after 8:30 AM on the same settlement date.

Source: ADB Cross-Border Settlement Infrastructure Forum (CSIF) Survey.

D. Indonesia

1. Market Size of Collective Investment Scheme

AUM (A)	GDP (G)	A/G (%)	No. of CIS	Note
USD5.52 billion	USD3,911.70 billion	0.14	2,544	Including discretionary CIS, PEFs, ETFs, REITs, and infrastructure CIS

AUM = assets under management, CIS = collective investment scheme, ETF = exchange-traded fund, GDP = gross domestic product, PEF = private equity fund, REIT = real estate investment trust.
Note: Information is as of the end of 2020.
Source: ADB Cross-Border Settlement Infrastructure Forum (CSIF) Survey.

2. Legal Structure of Collective Investment Scheme

Collective Investment Scheme Type	Open-end vs. Closed-end	Redeemable vs. Traded on Exchange	Investment Company vs. Unincorporated	Market Share (%)
Mutual fund	Open-end	Redeemable	CIS	89.4
ETF	Open-end	Traded on exchange	CIS	2.6
PEF	Open-end	Redeemable	CIS	5.0
REIT	Open-end	Redeemable	CIS	1.8
Infrastructure CIS	Open-end	Redeemable	CIS	1.2

CIS = collective investment scheme, ETF = exchange-traded fund, PEF = private equity fund, REIT = real estate investment trust.
Note: Information is as of the end of 2020.
Source: ADB Cross-Border Settlement Infrastructure Forum (CSIF) Survey.

3. Distribution Channel

Distribution Channel (%)				Electronic Platform Available?
Bank	Securities Company	Insurance Company	Others	
22.6	1.3		76.1	

Note: Information is as of the end of 2020.
Source: ADB Cross-Border Settlement Infrastructure Forum (CSIF) Survey.

4. Issuance of Collective Investment Scheme Unit

Service Coverage	Description
△	There are no certificates provided for unitholders. Only transaction report and confirmation, which can be represented in soft copy or hard copy format. For mutual funds, there are no certificates deposited at KSEI. S-INVEST only records the change in transactions and ownership. The mutual fund itself is deposited in a custodian bank.

KSEI = PT Kustodian Sentral Efek Indonesia (Indonesia Central Securities Depository).
Note: Information is as of the end of 2020.
Source: ADB Cross-Border Settlement Infrastructure Forum (CSIF) Survey.

5. Cross-Border Collective Investment Scheme Transactions

Home-Domiciled Collective Investment Scheme Sold Abroad (Outbound) Yes or No?	Foreign Collective Investment Schemes Sold in Your Economy (Inbound)
Yes	Cross-border transactions of CIS are not prohibited by law and such transaction-related deposit are carried out by custodian banks in Indonesia. The exception to the rule includes cross-border transactions that are related to establishing a local currency CIS in other economies or depositing the local currency CIS in offshore custodian banks.

CIS = collective investment scheme.
Note: Information is as of the end of 2020.
Source: ADB Cross-Border Settlement Infrastructure Forum (CSIF) Survey.

6. Central Platforms in Indonesia

Name of Central Platform	Operator	Model	ICSD Linkage
S-INVEST	KSEI	CSD Model	

CSD = central securities depository, ICSD = international central securities depository, KSEI = PT Kustodian Sentral Efek Indonesia (Indonesia Central Securities Depository).
Note: Information is as of the end of 2020.
Source: ADB Cross-Border Settlement Infrastructure Forum (CSIF) Survey.

Since 2016, the Indonesian CSD, PT Kustodian Sentral Efek Indonesia (KSEI), has launched and operated a central platform called S-INVEST to streamline, standardize, and monitor the post-trade processing of CIS. In September 2017, the Indonesian state regulator, OJK (Otoritas Jasa Keuangan—Indonesia Financial Services Authority), required the mandatory use of S-INVEST.[4] Currently, many distributors, asset management companies, and custodians utilize S-INVEST.

S-INVEST comprises four functional modules: (i) static data, (ii) order routing, (iii) post-trade processing, and (iv) reporting.

As for mutual funds, S-INVEST allows its users to perform the following tasks:

▶ Upon the request of the investor, the distributor,[5] or asset management company,[6] that is directly selling units can release a settlement instruction for subscription or redemption (on the T+0 settlement basis).

▶ The asset management company approves the settlement instruction.

▶ The custodian approves the settlement instruction.

▶ The custodian reflects the change in units and confirms the balance.

▶ And on T+1, the custodian calculates and provides the net asset value (NAV) in the system.

---

[4] Refer to the OJK Regulation No. 28/POJK.04/2016.
[5] A distributor is often called as a selling agent in Indonesia.
[6] An asset management company is often called an investment manager in Indonesia.

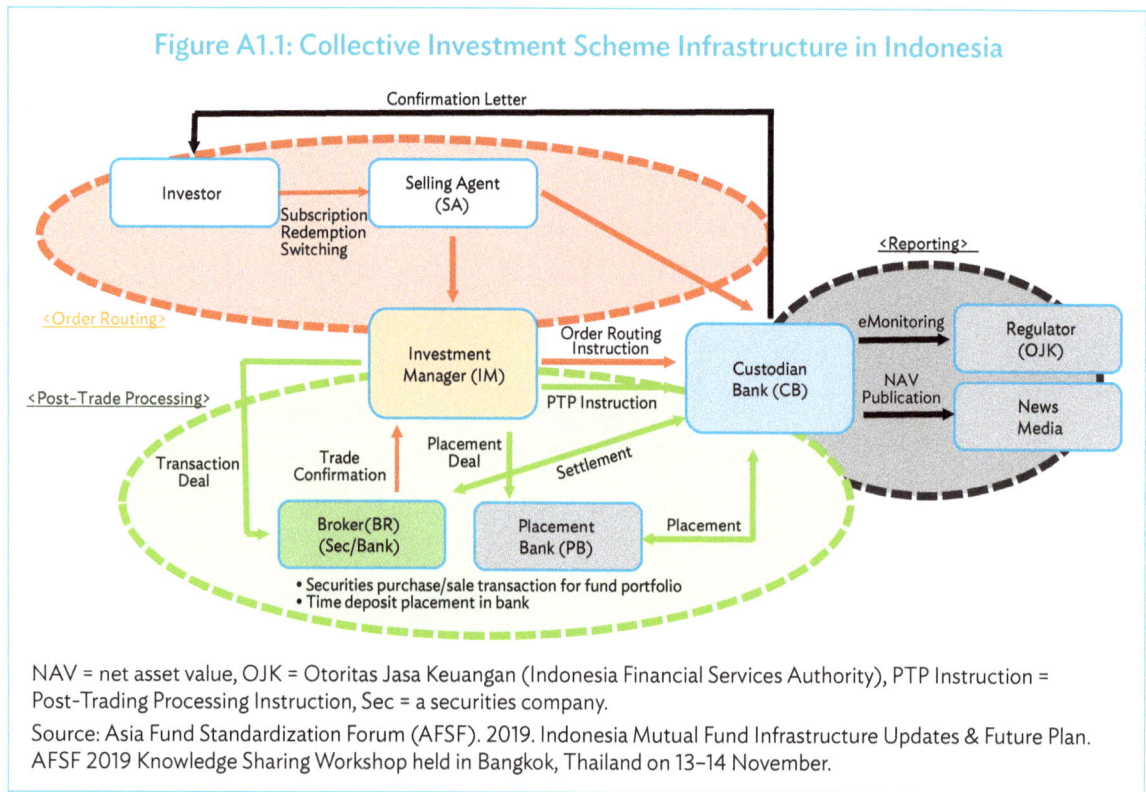

Figure A1.1: Collective Investment Scheme Infrastructure in Indonesia

NAV = net asset value, OJK = Otoritas Jasa Keuangan (Indonesia Financial Services Authority), PTP Instruction = Post-Trading Processing Instruction, Sec = a securities company.
Source: Asia Fund Standardization Forum (AFSF). 2019. Indonesia Mutual Fund Infrastructure Updates & Future Plan. AFSF 2019 Knowledge Sharing Workshop held in Bangkok, Thailand on 13–14 November.

7. *CIS Settlement Model and Completeness and Finality of Settlement*

Settlement of Subscription and Redemption

For order routing, the cash settlement for nonbank selling agents and fintech selling agents is carried out via the custodian banks' account in the designated bank. For subscription, investors need to transfer the cash from their account to the custodian banks' account in the specific banks. For redemption, custodian banks will transfer cash from CIS accounts to the investors' account in the bank.

The subscription process for bank selling agents utilizes central bank money through S-INVEST. For subscription, bank selling agents overbook the subscription cash from investor's account into pooling account. On T+1, bank transfers the cash from pooling account to respective CIS cash account under KSEI.

The transfer is conducted using the Bank Indonesia–Real Time Gross Settlement (BI-RTGS) and reflected on S-INVEST. Then, custodian banks withdraw the money from S-INVEST and transfer to the CIS account in each custodian bank. However, the redemption process for bank selling agents involves the same method as the case of nonbanks and fintech selling agents.

Legal Requirements on Settlement Completeness and Finality

Settlement completeness and finality is described in the POJK Regulation (No 22/POJK.04/2019) (Box A1.3).

Figure A1.2: Cash Transfer Flow of Subscription via Bank Indonesia–Real Time Gross Settlement

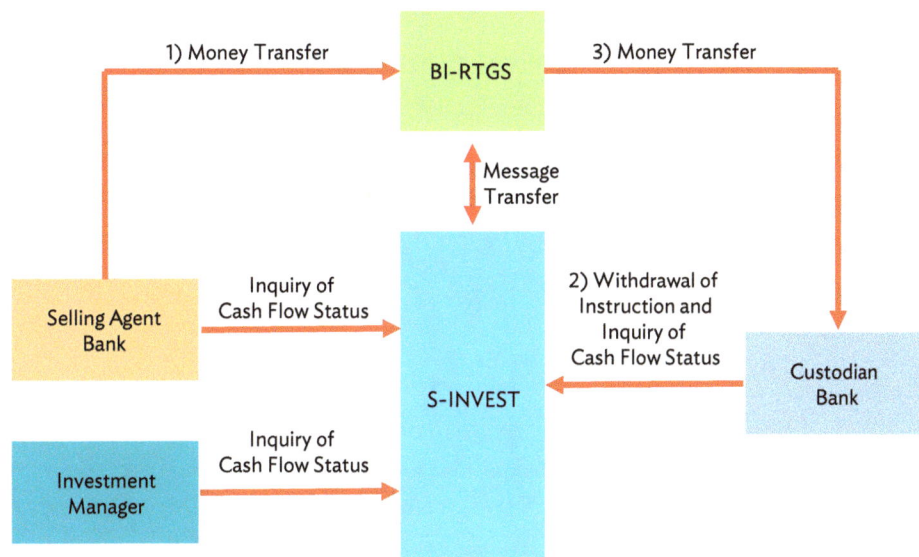

BI-RTGS = Bank Indonesia–Real Time Gross Settlement.
Source: ADB Cross-Border Settlement Infrastructure Forum (CSIF) Survey.

Box A1.3: POJK Regulation (No 22/POJK.04/2019)

Article 10
Securities Transaction Settlement, which has been conducted by:

▶ Central Securities Depository for the Securities Deposited in Central Securities Depository; the parties which conduct scrip securities transaction with valid deed of transfer;

▶ Clearing and Guarantee institution for futures contract and option;

▶ and custodian Bank for the investment product, which is not recorded and transacted in stock exchange, is deemed to be final and irrevocable.

Securities transaction settlement for government bonds are deemed to be final and irrevocable according to laws and regulations.

Article 11
Securities record in:

▶ Central Securities Depository in paperless form for the securities deposited in Central Securities Depository;

▶ Registrar or Issuers and/or Public Company, which conducts their own registration for scrip securities;

▶ Clearing and Guarantee Institution for the futures contract and option being transacted in stock exchange; and/or

▶ Custodian Bank for the investment products, which is not recorded or transacted in stock exchange, is evidence of a legal record of ownership for securities.

The recording of government bonds is conducted according to laws and regulations.

Source: ADB Cross-Border Settlement Infrastructure Forum (CSIF) Survey.

E. Republic of Korea

1. Market Size of Collective Investment Scheme

AUM (A)	GDP (G)	A/G (%)	No. of CIS	Note
USD577 billion	USD1,631 billion	35.3	14,346	

AUM = assets under management, CIS = collective investment scheme, GDP = gross domestic product, USD = United States dollar.
Note: Information is as of the end of 2020.
Source: ADB Cross-Border Settlement Infrastructure Forum (CSIF) Survey.

2. Legal Structure of Collective Investment Scheme

Collective Investment Scheme Type	Open-end vs. Closed-end	Redeemable vs. Traded on Exchange	Investment Company vs. Unincorporated	Market Share (%)
Unit trust	Open-end	Redeemable	Unincorporated	98.6
Investment company	Closed-end	Traded on exchange	Investment company	1.4

Note: Information is as of the end of 2020.
Source: ADB Cross-Border Settlement Infrastructure Forum (CSIF) Survey.

3. Distribution Channel

Distribution Channel (%)				Electronic Platform Available?
Bank	Securities Company	Insurance Company	Others	
39.44	55.55	1.93	3.08	

Note: Information is as of the end of 2020.
Source: ADB Cross-Border Settlement Infrastructure Forum (CSIF) Survey.

4. Issuance of Collective Investment Scheme Unit

Service Coverage	Description
O	All CIS units are electronically registered, not issued in a physical form. It is required by law to deposit CIS units at KSD (via FundNet).

CIS = collective investment scheme, KSD = Korea Securities Depository.
Note: Information is as of the end of 2020.
Source: ADB Cross-Border Settlement Infrastructure Forum (CSIF) Survey.

5.   *Cross-Border Collective Investment Scheme Transactions*

Home-Domiciled Collective Investment Scheme Sold Abroad (Outbound) Yes or No?	Foreign Collective Investment Schemes Sold in Your Economy (Inbound)		
	Yes or No	Data	Pertinent Laws
Yes	Yes	648 CIS, USD28.8 billion	Financial Investment Services and Capital Markets Act

CIS = collective investment scheme, USD = United States dollar.
Note: Information is as of August 2020.
Source: ADB Cross-Border Settlement Infrastructure Forum (CSIF) Survey.

6.   *Central Platforms in the Republic of Korea*

Name of Central Platform	Operator	Model	ICSD Linkage
FundNet	KSD	CSD Model	Euroclear Clearstream

CSD = central securities depository, ICSD = international central securities depository, KSD = Korea Securities Depository.
Note: Information is as of August 2020.
Source: ADB Cross-Border Settlement Infrastructure Forum (CSIF) Survey.

Since 2004, the Korea Securities Depository (KSD) launched and operated FundNet as a central platform for the local asset management industry. The subscription and redemption modules of FundNet are briefly described in Figure A1.3.

Figure A1.3: Functional Description of FundNet

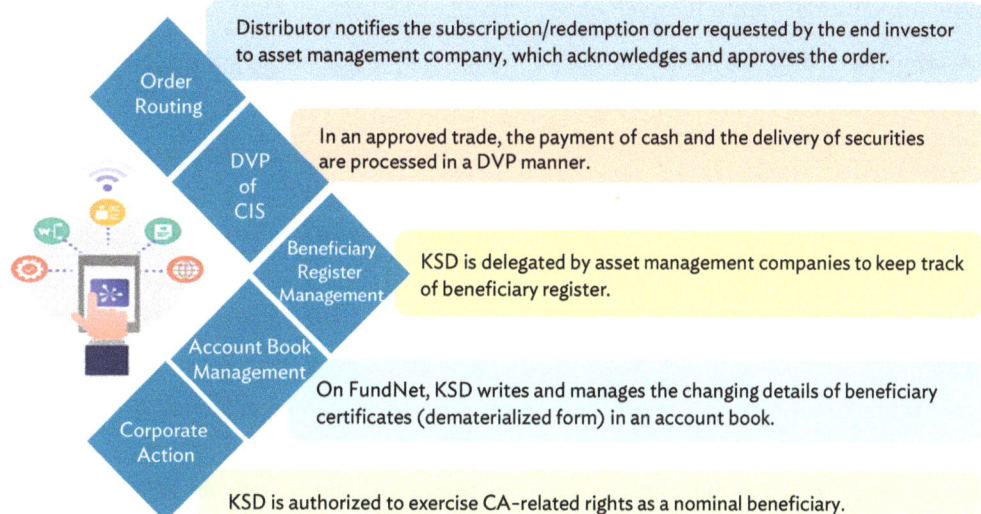

Distributor notifies the subscription/redemption order requested by the end investor to asset management company, which acknowledges and approves the order.

In an approved trade, the payment of cash and the delivery of securities are processed in a DVP manner.

KSD is delegated by asset management companies to keep track of beneficiary register.

On FundNet, KSD writes and manages the changing details of beneficiary certificates (dematerialized form) in an account book.

KSD is authorized to exercise CA-related rights as a nominal beneficiary.

Order Routing

DVP of CIS

Beneficiary Register Management

Account Book Management

Corporate Action

CA = corporate action, CIS = collective investment scheme, DVP = delivery versus payment, KSD = Korea Securities Depository.
Source: ADB Cross-Border Settlement Infrastructure Forum (CSIF) Survey.

Also, KSD supports the inbound transaction of European-domiciled Undertaking for Collective Investment in Transferable Securities collective investment scheme (UCITS CIS) by processing subscription and redemption via the linkage between FundNet and ICSD platforms (Euroclear's FundSettle and Clearstream's Vestima).

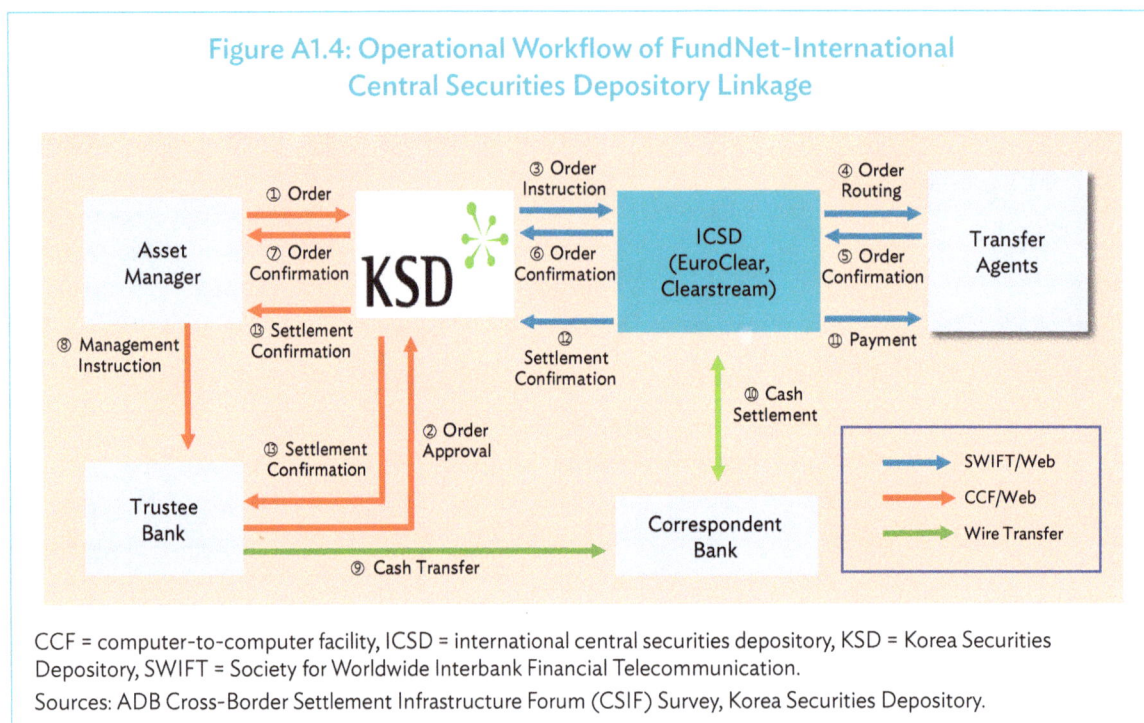

Figure A1.4: Operational Workflow of FundNet-International Central Securities Depository Linkage

CCF = computer-to-computer facility, ICSD = international central securities depository, KSD = Korea Securities Depository, SWIFT = Society for Worldwide Interbank Financial Telecommunication.
Sources: ADB Cross-Border Settlement Infrastructure Forum (CSIF) Survey, Korea Securities Depository.

To engage in offshore CIS transactions, FundNet users should sign a service agreement for offshore CIS transaction, the essential details of which are as follows:

(i) Among users, only asset management companies or trustees can apply for the service.

(ii) Scope of Service
 • Account opening on the ICSD level under KSD's nominee account upon the request of user.
 • Order routing to ICSD and confirmation of order receipt.
 • Sharing of balance information.
 • Notification of corporation actions.

(iii) Under the agreement, service users are charged with fees related to transaction (ordering and settlement) cash transfer, asset custody, reporting, and corporate action processing.[7]

For offshore transactions, KSD linked FundNet with Fundsettle (Euroclear) in 2012 and with Vestima (Clearstream) in 2015. Albeit not mandatory, the CSD-ICSD linkage service is well received by many Korean asset managers since the service fees are very reasonable (from which KSD takes no margin)

---

[7] Transaction fee is known to be EUR5.

and KSD directly communicates with Euroclear and Clearstream, which are broadly connected to major transfer agents in Europe. However, as for non-UCITS CIS such as US-domiciled CIS or Asian CIS, KSD is currently reaching out to platform providers including fintech firms that offer disruptive solutions to drive down transaction costs and step up market accessibility.

Table A1.2: Size of Cross-Border Transactions

Cross-Border Transaction	Number of Collective Investment Scheme	Asset under Management (USD billion)	Note
Inbound	648	28.8	
Outbound	–	–	

USD = United States dollar.
Note: Information is as of the end of 2020.
Source: Korea Securities Depository.

7.   CIS Settlement Model and Completeness and Finality of Settlement

Settlement of Subscription and Redemption

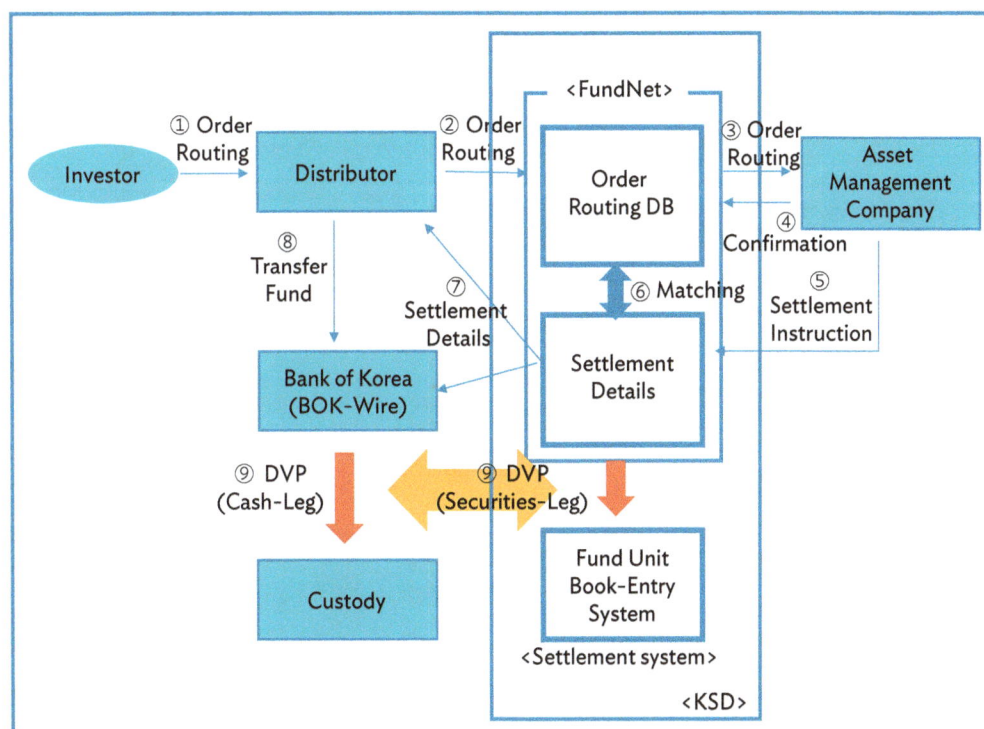

Figure A1.5: Collective Investment Scheme Settlement via FundNet

BOK = Bank of Korea, DB = database, DVP = delivery versus payment, KSD = Korea Securities Depository, RTGS = real-time gross settlement.
Note: BOK-Wire is an RTGS system for large-value payment system run by the BOK.
Source: ADB Cross-Border Settlement Infrastructure Forum (CSIF) Survey.

For CIS units, the operational workflow of delivery versus payment (DVP) settlement is as follows:

- Confirmation of Settlement Data (Process ①~⑤ as described in Figure A1.5): The order routed by the distributor is acknowledged and confirmed by the asset management company, which releases a settlement instruction (SI).
- Notification of Settlement Data (Process ⑦): SI is relayed via KSD to the distributor and trustee.
- Precondition for Cash Settlement (Process ⑧): In general, the distributor wires the corresponding money to its cash account in the RTGS of the Bank of Korea (BOK-WIRE).
- Confirmation of DVP Settlement Requirements: Once the cash arrives at the BOK-WIRE account (Process ⑧) and SI is confirmed (Process ⑥), an instruction is made to execute simultaneous settlement.
- Execution of DVP Settlement: DVP settlement comprises two legs (cash and securities) as above. Due to the irrevocability of settlement, once executed, trade settlement cannot be canceled.
- Cash-leg: The cash parking in the BOK-WIRE account should be wired to the trustee's account.
- Securities-leg: CIS units should be issued in the issuer's account at KSD (where the increase or decrease in the number of units is recorded).

As a Securities Settlement System (SSS) for CIS, KSD guarantees the completeness, finality, and irrevocability of settlement by operating its SSS in connection with BOK-WIRE.

Legal Requirements on Settlement Completeness

In the Republic of Korea, the Financial Investment Services and Capital Markets Act prescribes the legal effect of statement in KSD's participant account book as below, Box A1.4. It can be construed that settlement is completed once the details in the participant account are changed according to the trade.

Legal Requirements on Settlement Finality and Irrevocability

The Special Rules Concerning Payment and Settlement System of the Debtor Rehabilitation and Bankruptcy Act specifies that it is impossible for an insolvency administrator to nullify a trade that is already settled by an SSS appointed by the Korean financial authorities, such as the settlement system of KSD—a solid legal foundation for settlement finality.

Box A1.4: Financial Investment Services and Capital Markets Act

Article 311. Effect of Statement in Account Book
Securities Transaction Settlement, which has been conducted by

(1) Any person who is stated in an investor's account book and the participant's account book shall be deemed to hold the respective securities.

(2) Where a transfer between accounts is stated for the purpose of a transfer of securities in an investor's account book or participant's account book or where securities are stated to be pledged for the purpose of a creation of pledge and such pledgees are stated in such account books, securities shall be deemed to have been delivered.

Source: ADB Cross-Border Settlement Infrastructure Forum (CSIF) Survey.

F. Japan

1. *Market Size and Legal Structure of CIS*

Item Type	Total Net Assets (JPY million)	Compared with Previous Term (JPY million)	Number of CIS
Investment Trusts	257,846,292	4,172,602	13,498
Publicly Offered Investment Trusts	150,227,223	3,741,960	5,982
Contractual Type	139,431,074	3,706,123	5,913
Securities Investment Trust	139,431,074	3,706,123	5,913
Stock Investment Trusts	125,161,702	3,341,858	5,815
Unit Type	700,663	▲ 17,612	136
Open Type	124,461,040	3,359,470	5,679
ETF	54,807,831	1,548,915	192
Others	69,653,209	1,810,555	5,487
Bond Investment Trusts	14,269,372	364,265	98
Unit Type	2,557	▲ 25	11
Open Type	14,266,814	364,290	87
MRF (Money Reserve Fund)	13,662,602	364,283	12
MMF (Money Market Fund)	0	0	0
Others	604,213	7	75
Investment Trusts Other Than Securities Investment Trusts	0	0	0
Money Trust Benefits Fund	0	0	0
Investment Trusts Managed by Trustee	0	0	0
Investment Companies	10,796,149	35,837	69
Securities Investment Companies	0	0	0
Real Estate Investment Companies	10,711,933	36,001	62
Infrastructure CIS	84,216	▲ 164	7
Privately Placed Investment Trusts	107,619,069	430,642	7,516
Contractual Type	105,232,733	393,351	7,476
Securities Investment Trusts	105,232,733	393,351	7,476
Stock Investment Trusts	100,351,179	201,258	6,194
Bond Investment Trusts	4,881,554	192,093	1,282
Investment Trusts Other Than Securities Investment Trusts	0	0	0
Investment Trusts Managed by Trustee	0	0	0
Investment Companies	2,386,336	37,291	40
Securities Investment Companies	0	0	0
Real Estate Investment Companies	2,386,336	37,291	40

CIS = collective investment scheme, ETF = exchange-traded fund, JPY = Japanese yen.
Note: Information is as of the end of 2020.
Source: ADB Cross-Border Settlement Infrastructure Forum (CSIF) Survey.

2.   Distribution Channel

Distribution Channel (%)				Electronic Platform Available?
Bank	Securities Company	Insurance Company	Others	
46.25	50.90		2.85	

Note: Information is as of the end of 2020.
Source: ADB Cross-Border Settlement Infrastructure Forum (CSIF) Survey.

3.   Central Platforms in Japan

Name of Central Platform	Operator	Model	ICSD Linkage
BETS (Book-Entry Transfer System)	JASDEC	CSD Model	

BETS = Book-Entry Transfer System, CSD = central securities depository, ICSD = international central securities depository, JASDEC = Japan Securities Depository Center.
Note: Information is as of the end of 2020.
Source: ADB Cross-Border Settlement Infrastructure Forum (CSIF) Survey.

The Japan Securities Depository Center (JASDEC) runs Book-Entry Transfer System (BETS) to execute the DVP settlement of CIS subscription and redemption.[8]

BETS was launched in January 2007 as a central platform for post-trade processing of subscription and redemption in operational connection with the Bank of Japan for cash-leg settlement.

Figure A1.6: Collective Investment Scheme Settlement via Book-Entry Transfer System

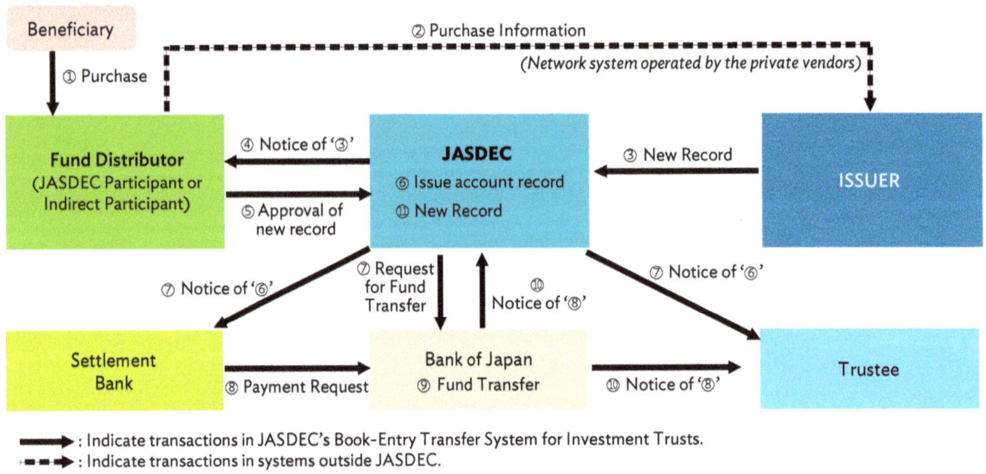

JASDEC = Japan Securities Depository Center.
Source: ADB Cross-Border Settlement Infrastructure Forum (CSIF) Survey.

[8]   JASDEC. 2015. *Book-Entry Transfer System for Investment Trusts in Japan.* Presented at the Asia-Pacific CSD Group (ACG) 19 on 3–6 November in Taipei,China.

The benefits of BETS include the saving of costs and time for subscription and redemption, the prevention of loss, damage, forgery, and theft of physical certificates; and the daily reconciliation between distributors and asset managers.

G. Lao People's Democratic Republic

1. Market Size of CIS

Currently, there are no mutual funds issued in the capital market of the Lao People's Democratic Republic (Lao PDR). However, the provision on mutual funds is mentioned in the Law on Securities. Also, there is the Decision on Mutual Funds issued in 2019.

2. Issuance of Collective Investment Scheme Unit

Service Coverage	Description
X	From the date when CIS units are offered and distributed, the asset management company shall issue a physical beneficiary certificate to the subscriber.
	It is not required by law to deposit CIS units at a CSD.

CIS = collective investment scheme, CSD = central securities depository.
Note: Information is as of the end of 2020.
Source: ADB Cross-Border Settlement Infrastructure Forum (CSIF) Survey.

H. Hong Kong, China

1. Market Size of Collective Investment Scheme

AUM (A)	GDP (G)	A/G (%)	No. of Unit Trust and Mutual Fund	No. of Authorized Collective Investment Schemes (Total)
USD1,995 billion	–	580	2,194	2,789

AUM = assets under management, GDP = gross domestic product.
Notes: A/G (580%) is in terms of both Hong Kong, China- and non-Hong Kong, China-domiciled authorized funds.
Information is as of the end of 2020.
Source: ADB Cross-Border Settlement Infrastructure Forum (CSIF) Survey.

2. Legal Structure of Collective Investment Scheme

Unit Trusts and Mutual Funds Hong Kong, China Domiciled	Unit Trusts and Mutual Funds Non-Hong Kong, China Domiciled	REITs	Investment-linked Assurance Schemes	Pooled Retirement CIS	MPF Master Trust Schemes	MPF Pooled Investment CIS	Paper Gold Schemes	Total
810	1,384	12	300	33	27	210	13	2,789

CIS = collective investment schemes, MPF = Mandatory Provident Fund, REITs = real estate investment trusts.
Note: Information is as of the end of 2020.
Source: ADB Cross-Border Settlement Infrastructure Forum (CSIF) Survey.

3. Issuance of Collective Investment Scheme Unit

Service Coverage	Description
X	It is not required by law to deposit CIS units at CSD.

CIS = collective investment scheme, CSD = central securities depository.
Note: Information is as of the end of 2020.
Source: ADB Cross-Border Settlement Infrastructure Forum Survey.

4. Cross-Border Collective Investment Scheme Transactions

Number of Funds by Origin	As of 31 December 2020	As of 31 March 2020	Change (%)	As of 31 December 2019	Year-Over-Year Change (%)
Luxembourg	1,034	1,032	0.2	1,041	−0.7
Ireland	237	222	6.8	220	7.7
United Kingdom	34	37	−8.1	51	−33.3
Other Europe	0	0	N/A	3	−100
People's Republic of China	51	50	2	50	2
Bermuda	1	1	0	1	0
Cayman Islands	22	26	−15.4	30	−26.7
Others	5	5	0	6	−16.7
Total	1,384	1,373	0.8	1,402	−1.3

Source: ADB Cross-Border Settlement Infrastructure Forum Survey.

5. Central Platforms in Hong Kong, China

Name of Central Platform	Operator	Model	ICSD Linkage
Fund Order Routing and Settlement Service	HKMA	CSD Model	

CSD = central securities depository, HKMA = Hong Kong Monetary Authority, ICSD = international central securities depository.
Source: ADB Cross-Border Settlement Infrastructure Forum Survey.

Since 11 August 2009, the Hong Kong Monetary Authority (HKMA) has launched and operated a central platform, the Central Moneymarkets Unit Fund Order Routing and Settlement Service (CMU FORS), in order to automate and standardize the complex and fragmented post-trade space of Hong Kong, China.

FORS was designed to support both domestic and cross-border transaction of Hong Kong, China by enabling distributors, asset managers, custodians, and other market players to place, route, and settle orders and safely keep assets on the central platform in a standardized manner. The scope of platform services includes

▶ handling subscription, redemption, and switching orders;

▶ generating corresponding confirmation and payment instructions; and

▶ providing regular reports, and settlement and custody of CIS.

Distributors can fully or selectively use FORS to suit their needs. For instance, they can simply route orders via HKMA to transfer agents or use the full service, which processes both order routing and settlement.[9]

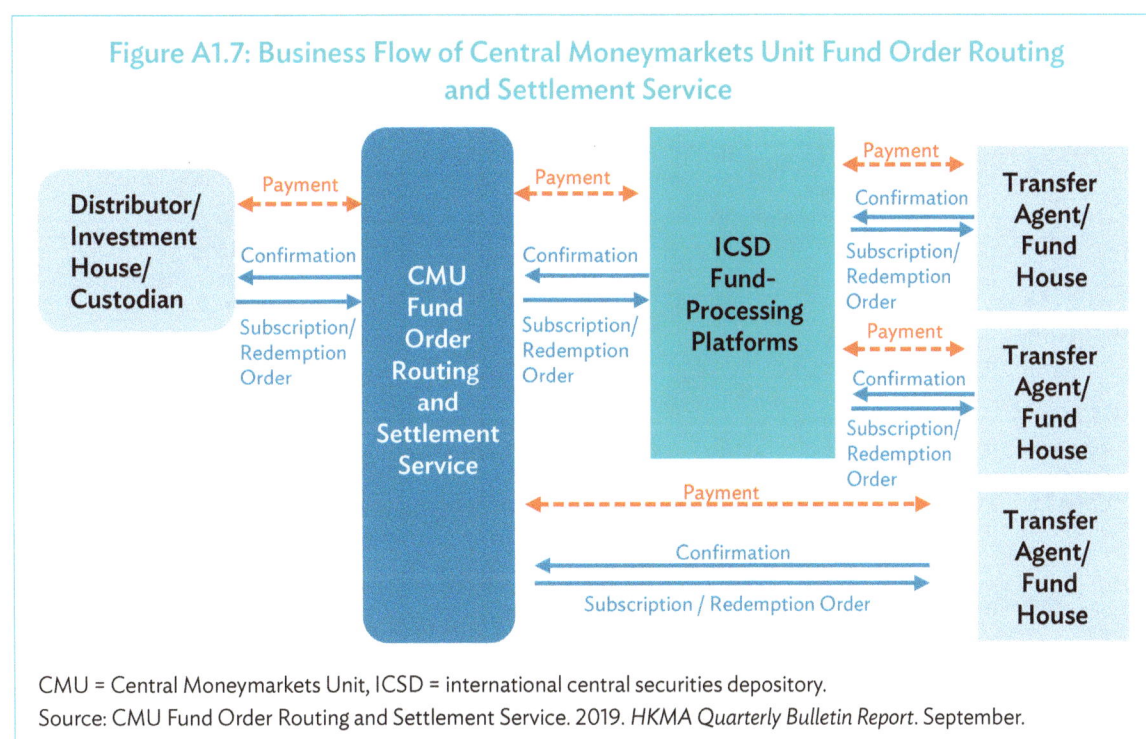

Figure A1.7: Business Flow of Central Moneymarkets Unit Fund Order Routing and Settlement Service

CMU = Central Moneymarkets Unit, ICSD = international central securities depository.
Source: CMU Fund Order Routing and Settlement Service. 2019. *HKMA Quarterly Bulletin Report*. September.

Settlement instructions are executed in straight-through-processing (STP) manner. Automatically generated under the name of the distributor, settlement Instructions are delivered to transfer agents while the cash-leg settlement is processed by CMU FORS and a multi-currency payment platform called Clearing House Automated Transfer System (CHATS). The cash accounts of participants are not managed by FORS.

As CMU FORS has a seamless interface with the Hong Kong dollar, US dollar, euro, and renminbi RTGS systems (i.e., HKD CHATS, USD CHATS, Euro CHATS, and RMB CHATS) in Hong Kong, China. Cash transfers related to securities transactions can be effected through the banks' settlement accounts of the respective currency maintained with settlement instructions or a clearing bank.

---

[9]   In this case, the cash settlement is done outside CMU in the method preferred by the distributor.

In addition, HKMA links up with ICSD platforms to provide an STP that enables investors to access offshore CIS, such as UCITS CIS.

CMU FORS effectively serves as a hub for the post-trade processing between the buy-side (e.g., distributors and custodians) and sell-side (e.g., transfer agents and fund houses[10]) of CIS investing by making it possible for users to communicate with each other regardless of their differing messaging types such as File Transfer Service, SWIFT, or authenticated fax.

Figure A1.8: Central Moneymarkets Unit Delivery versus Payment Settlement

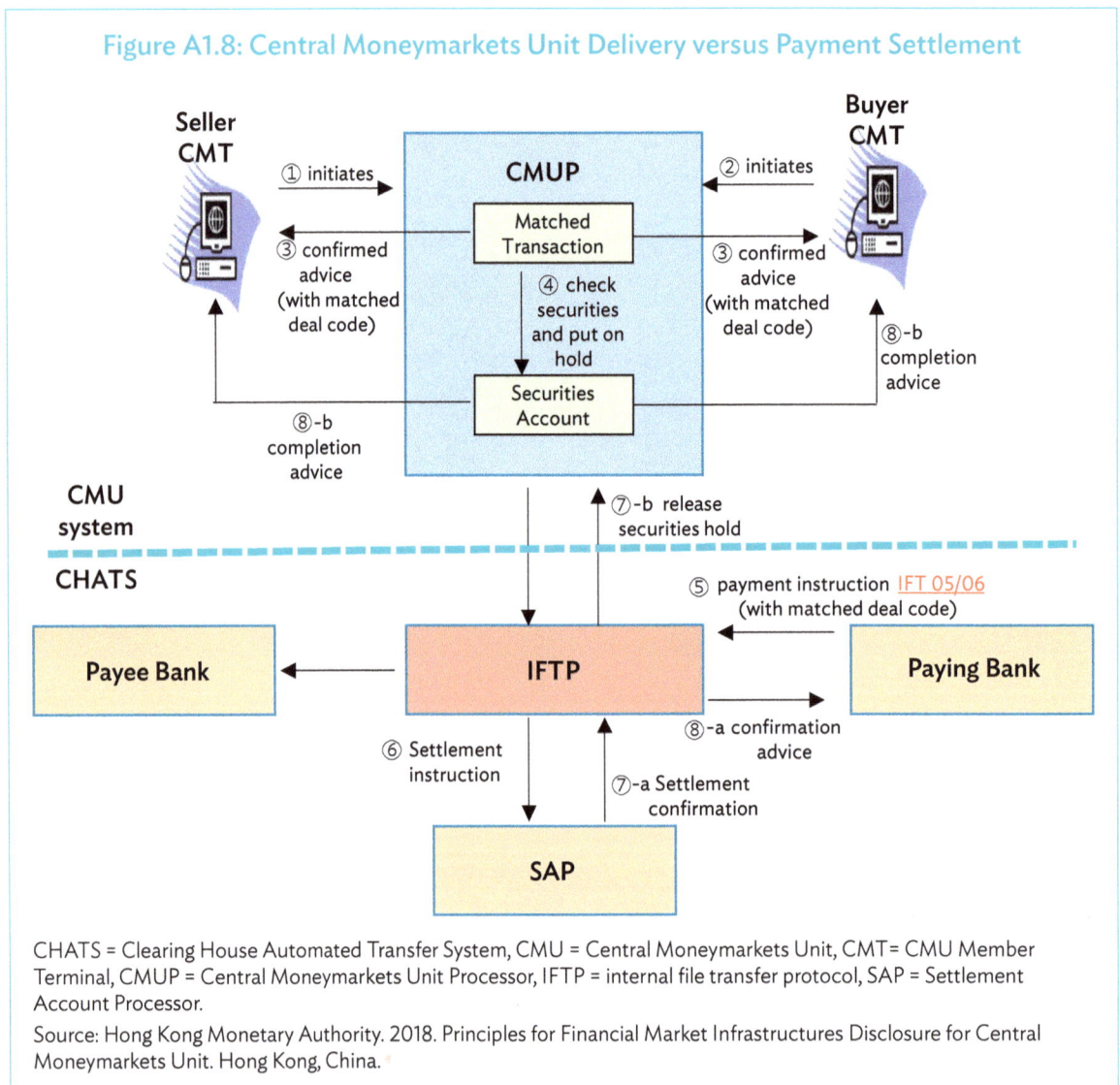

CHATS = Clearing House Automated Transfer System, CMU = Central Moneymarkets Unit, CMT = CMU Member Terminal, CMUP = Central Moneymarkets Unit Processor, IFTP = internal file transfer protocol, SAP = Settlement Account Processor.
Source: Hong Kong Monetary Authority. 2018. Principles for Financial Market Infrastructures Disclosure for Central Moneymarkets Unit. Hong Kong, China.

---

[10] "Fund house" is a frequently used jargon in the CIS industry referring to asset management companies.

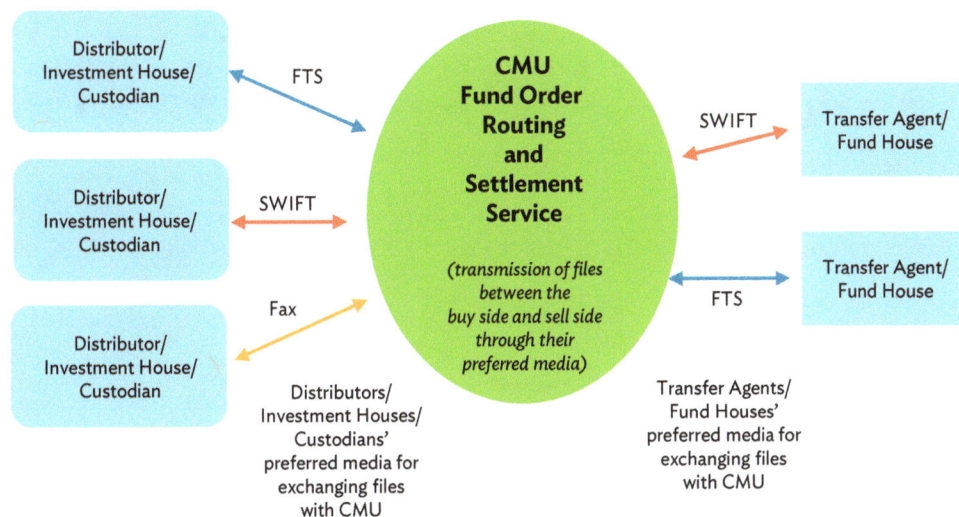

Figure A1.9: Multiple Communications Channels Supported by Central Moneymarkets Unit Fund Order Routing and Settlement Service

CMU = Central Moneymarkets Unit, FTS = File Transfer Service, SWIFT = Society for Worldwide Interbank Financial Telecommunication.

Source: Hong Kong Monetary Authority. 2009. CMU Fund Order Routing and Settlement Service. Hong Kong, China.

6. CIS Settlement Model and Completeness and Finality of Settlement

Legal Requirements on Settlement Completeness

All transfers of title within designated financial market infrastructures (FMIs) are effected by debiting the relevant account of the transferor and crediting the relevant account of the transferee. This is provided in the rules and procedures of the FMIs.

As a condition of participation in the designated FMI, participants are obliged to comply with the Rules and Procedures, which are governed by and construed in accordance with the laws of Hong Kong, China.

Legal Requirements on Settlement Finality and Irrevocability

FMIs deemed designated under the Payment Systems and Stored Value Facilities Ordinance issue a certificate of finality. The Payment Systems and Stored Value Facilities Ordinance provides statutory protection of the transfer orders settled through the system from the insolvency and other laws in Hong Kong, China and, where private international law rules of Hong Kong, China are applicable, from the equivalent laws of a place outside Hong Kong, China.

The CMU Fund Order Routing system ensures that transfer orders settled through the system are irrevocable and will not be reversed by the insolvency of a participant, whereas any rights resulting from the underlying transaction of any such transfer order will be preserved.

Therefore, all transactions settled through the system are irrevocable and final, and enjoy statutory backing to settlement finality. Once a payment is debited or credited to the settlement account, it shall be deemed made, completed, irrevocable, and final regardless of the nature of the payment.

I.   Malaysia

1.   Market Size of Collective Investment Scheme

AUM (A)	GDP (G)	A/G (%)	No. of CIS	Note
130 (MYR522.68 billion)			718	Reflecting total NAV and the number of CIS offered to retail investors (e.g., unit trusts, ETFs, and closed-end CIS).

AUM = assets under management, CIS = collective investment scheme, ETF = exchange-traded fund, GDP = gross domestic product, MYR = Malaysian ringgit, NAV = net asset value.
Note: Information is as of the end of 2020.
Source: ADB Cross-Border Settlement Infrastructure Forum (CSIF) Survey.

2.   Legal Structure of Collective Investment Scheme

Collective Investment Scheme Type	Open-end vs. Closed-end	Redeemable vs. Traded on Exchange	Investment Company vs. Unincorporated	Market Share (%)
Unit trust	Open-end	Redeemable	Unincorporated	99.40
ETF	Open-end	Traded on exchange	Unincorporated	0.42
Closed-end CIS	Closed-end	Traded on exchange	Investment company	0.08

CIS = collective investment schemes, ETF = exchange-traded fund.
Note: Information is as of the end of 2020.
Source: ADB Cross-Border Settlement Infrastructure Forum (CSIF) Survey.

3.   Distribution Channel of Collective Investment Schemes

Distribution Channel (%)				Electronic Platform Available?
Bank	Securities Company	Insurance Company	Others	
18.66	0.08		81.26	Yes

Note: Information is as of the end of 2020.
Source: ADB Cross-Border Settlement Infrastructure Forum (CSIF) Survey.

4.   Issuance of Collective Investment Scheme Unit

Service Coverage	Description
X	For subscription, an asset management company is not required to issue a physical beneficiary certificate to the investor. However, a receipt is issued to investors to confirm the subscription. The receipt would typically contain, among others, the CIS name, trade date, amount received, sales charges, investment amount, units credited, and net asset value per unit. It is not required by law to deposit CIS units at CSD. The issuance of physical beneficiary certificates is not mandatory.

CIS = collective investment scheme, CSD = central securities depository.
Note: Information is as of the end of 2020.
Source: ADB Cross-Border Settlement Infrastructure Forum (CSIF) Survey.

5. Cross-Border Collective Investment Scheme Transactions

Home-Domiciled Collective Investment Scheme Sold Abroad (Outbound) Yes or No?	Foreign Collective Investment Schemes Sold in Your Economy (Inbound)		
	Yes or No	Data	Pertinent Laws
Yes	Yes	2 CIS (MYR0.51 billion)	Capital Markets and Services Act, 2007

CIS = collective investment scheme, MYR = Malaysian ringgit.
Note: Information is as of the end of 2020.
Source: ADB Cross-Border Settlement Infrastructure Forum (CSIF) Survey.

6. CIS Settlement Model and Completeness and Finality of Settlement

Settlement of Subscription and Redemption

In Malaysia, settlement does not involve the central bank's RTGS. As for subscription to CIS units, investors deposit cash into a collection account (e.g., a bank account designated as trust account with a licensed bank) of asset manager such as a unit trust management company (hereinafter UTMC). Then, the UTMC will instruct trustee to create CIS units stating the number of units to be created.

The UTMC is required to pay the trustee the value of units created within 10 days of giving instructions from the collection account.

Settlement of ASEAN Collective Investment Scheme in Malaysia

The settlement of ASEAN CIS is not performed differently from any other CIS subscription. When a request for CIS subscription is received from an investor, payments for the subscriptions must be from the investor (within a specific timeline, depending on each CIS but typically within T+3) directly to the home economy manager/UTMC's collection account.

Proceeds and payments received in the manager's collection accounts will be used to pay for the creation of units to trustee that will take place within 10 days. No beneficiary certificate is issued for subscription.

J. Philippines

1. Market Size of Collective Investment Scheme

AUM (A)	GDP (G)	A/G (%)	No. of CIS	Note
USD20.50 billion (PHP993.50 billion)			251 UITFs	

AUM = assets under management, CIS = collective investment scheme, GDP = gross domestic product, PHP = Philippine peso, UITFs = unit investment trust funds.
Note: Information is as of the end of 2020.
Source: ADB Cross-Border Settlement Infrastructure Forum (CSIF) Survey.

There are two types of CIS in the Philippines that are regulated by different regulatory authorities. These are mutual funds (investment companies) supervised by the Securities and Exchange Commission (SEC) and unit investment trust funds (UITFs) supervised by the Bangko Sentral ng Pilipinas (BSP).

UITFs are issued by BSP-supervised financial institutions with trust licenses and are offered to the investing public in the form of unit participation. UITFs are not registered with the BSP but are subject to prior BSP approval before it can be offered.

2.   *Legal Structure of Collective Investment Scheme*

Collective Investment Scheme Type	Open-end vs. Closed-end	Redeemable vs. Traded on Exchange	Investment Company vs. Unincorporated	Market Share (%)
UITFs	Open-end	Redeemable	Unincorporated	–

– = not available, UITFs = unit investment trust funds.
Note: Information is as of the end of 2020.
Source: ADB Cross-Border Settlement Infrastructure Forum (CSIF) Survey.

3.   *Source Distribution Channel*

	Distribution Channel (%)	
TDs of Banks and NBFIs	**Trust Corporations**	**Sum**
70.44	29.56	100.00

TD = Trust Department, NBFIs = nonbank financial institutions.
Note: Information is as of the end of 2020.
Source: ADB Cross-Border Settlement Infrastructure Forum (CSIF) Survey.

In the case of the Philippines, UITFs may be distributed by banks, trust corporations, and nonbank financial institutions (NBFIs) with trust licenses (such as investment houses). As of the third quarter of 2020, UITFs that are offered by trust corporations and trust departments of banks and/or NBFIs are as above.

4.   *Issuance of Collective Investment Scheme Unit*

Service Coverage	Description
X	Once the subscription has been approved and settled by the trust entity, the beneficial owner shall receive a confirmation of participation (COP). The COP, which can either be in electronic or hard copy, is kept by the UITF account owner.
	COPs for UITFs are not required to be deposited in a CSD.

CSD = central securities depository, UITFs = unit investment trust funds.
Note: Information is as of the end of 2020.
Source: ADB Cross-Border Settlement Infrastructure Forum (CSIF) Survey.

5.   *Cross-Border Collective Investment Scheme Transaction*

Home-Domiciled Collective Investment Scheme Sold Abroad (Outbound) Yes or No?	Foreign Collective Investment Schemes Sold in Your Economy (Inbound)		
	Yes or No	Data	Pertinent Laws
Yes	Yes		

Note: Information is as of the end of 2020.
Source: ADB Cross-Border Settlement Infrastructure Forum (CSIF) Survey.

Foreign funds are sold in the local market through feeder fund or fund-of-fund UITF structures.[11] Under this structure, the local fund (referred to as the investor fund) invests in the foreign fund (also referred to as the target fund). This arrangement provides the local investors access to the foreign fund.

The current BSP regulations allow foreign funds to be sold domestically through feeder fund and fund-of-fund structures of UITFs. Under this framework, the local fund (referred to as the investor fund) invests in the foreign fund (also referred to as the target fund). This arrangement provides the local investors access to the foreign fund.

The BSP concurs on the expectation of growth in cross-border transactions in view of the admission of the SEC of the Philippines to the ASEAN CIS Framework and the SEC's subsequent issuance of the "Rules on Authorization of an Investment Company as a Qualifying CIS and Recognition of a Foreign CIS under the ASEAN CIS Framework." Thus, growth may be observed in outbound transactions involving mutual funds (which are the CIS regulated by the SEC) and inbound transactions from ASEAN CIS member states.

6.   *Central Platforms in Philippines*

The referenced models (e.g., Central Securities Depository [CSD] Model, Transfer Agent [TA] Model, or International Central Securities Depository [ICSD] Model) have not been implemented in the Philippines. Subscriptions and/or redemptions of UITFs are not performed by a CSD. Instead, these are directly processed by the trust entities offering UITFs. Nonetheless, the purchases and sales of the underlying assets of a UITF are coursed through securities dealers and/or brokers, which maintain accounts with a CSD.

As noted in the BSP's April 2021 response to the survey on linkage to ICSDs, the trustee and/or issuer of a UITF invested in foreign funds maintains an account with a foreign custodian. Holdings are lodged either under the name of the trust entity in an omnibus account structure, or under the name of the trust department in a specific sub-account.

---

[11]   A trust entity refers to a (1) bank or a nonbank financial institution, through its specifically designated business unit to perform trust functions; or (2) trust corporation, authorized by the BSP to engage in trust and other fiduciary business under Section 79 of Republic Act No. 8791 or to perform investment management services under Section 53 of the Act.

7.   Collective Investment Scheme Subscription and/or Redemption

The subscription of UITFs does not involve a CSD. Nevertheless, the purchases and sales of the underlying assets of a UITF are coursed through securities dealers and/or brokers. The latter maintains the accounts with a CSD.

In the case of ICSD, the trustee and/or issuer of UITFs maintains an account with foreign custodian. The account could be under the name of the supervised institution under an omnibus account structure, or with sub-accounts for the trust departments.

8.   Collective Investment Scheme Settlement Model and Completeness and Finality of Settlement

Settlement of Subscription and Redemption

In the Philippines, the settlement of securities is completed via DVP, meaning that the delivery of securities is conditional on the availability of CIS needed for settlement. Then, the transfer agent and/or registry records the ownership of securities in its books and/or system.

Similarly, the subscription to UITFs (one of the CIS types in the Philippines) is consummated upon payment of the subscription amount by the clients. The trust entity, likewise, records the corresponding units of participation in its books and/or system and issue certificate of participation to clients as evidence of their subscriptions to the UITF.

The legal grounds for securities settlement in the Philippines are presented in Box A1.5.

Box A1.5: Regulation Code (SRC) (Republic Act 8799)

2015 Implementing Rules and Regulations of the Securities

3.1.25. Transfer agent is any person who performs on behalf of an issuer or by itself as issuer any of the following activities:

3.1.25.3. Registers the transfer of such securities.

3.1.25.5. Records the ownership of securities by bookkeeping entry without physical issuance of securities certificates.

36.4.1.7. The procedures of a transfer agent are binding on and enforceable against issuers for which they act, registered securities holders and transferees who present securities for transfer. To minimize the issuance and movement of and to facilitate other dealings with those securities eligible to the operations of a registered clearing agency, a transfer agent and registered clearing agency shall jointly formulate and abide by written procedures addressing certificated and uncertificated securities issuance, transfers, cancellations, registration, confirmation and reconciliation of positions in securities, audit, replacement of lost securities, signature guarantees, delivery processes and turnaround times.

36.4.4. Clearing and Settlement

36.4.4.1. Exchanges and other transaction markets shall ensure that the clearing and settlement arrangement in the exchange of assets subject of the trade shall be on a DVP scheme such that delivery of the securities occurs if and only if payment occurs.

36.4.4.5. The Securities and Exchange Commission may require market participants to use uniform settlement systems in the public interest and for the protection of the investors including the use of a central counterparty (CCP) in the clearing and settlement of trades in all markets.

Rule 44—Records of Clearing Agencies

44.1. All transactions between clearing agency and its participants must be recorded by book entries.

44.2. The corporate secretary's or the stock transfer agent's receipt of the report of such transactions from a clearing agency shall be deemed a recording by the corporate secretary or the transfer agent of the transactions in the books of the corporation.

49.2.10. Delivery of Securities

Nothing in this rule shall be construed as affecting the absolute right of a customer of a broker-dealer to receive in the course of normal business operations following demand made on the broker-dealer, the physical delivery of certificates for:

49.2.10.1. Fully paid securities to which he is entitled, and

49.2.12.3. Fully paid securities shall include all securities carried for the account of a customer in a cash account or a margin account if they have been fully paid for; provided, however, that the term "fully paid securities" shall not apply to any securities which are purchased in transactions for which the customer has not made full payment.

Source: ADB Cross-Border Settlement Infrastructure Forum (CSIF) Survey.

K. Singapore

1. Market Size of Collective Investment Scheme

AUM (A)	GDP (G)	A/G (%)	No. of CIS	Note
SGD2,946 billion	SGD376 billion	786	N/A	

AUM = assets under management, CIS = collective investment scheme, GDP = gross domestic product, N/A = not applicable, SGD = Singapore dollar.
Note: Information is as of the end of 2020.
Source: ADB Cross-Border Settlement Infrastructure Forum (CSIF) Survey.

2. Legal Structure of Collective Investment Scheme

Collective Investment Scheme Type	Open-end vs. Closed-end	Redeemable vs. Traded on Exchange	Investment company vs. Unincorporated
Unit trust	Open-end	Redeemable	Unincorporated
		Trade on exchange	
Unit trusts (REITs)	Closed-end	Trade on exchange	Unincorporated
Unit trusts	Closed-end	Trade on exchange	Unincorporated
Limited partnerships	Open-end	Redeemable	Unincorporated
Limited partnerships	Closed-end	Not redeemable or exchange traded	Unincorporated
Variable capital company	Open-end	Redeemable	Corporate
Variable capital company	Closed-end	Not redeemable or exchange traded	Corporate

REITs = real estate investment trusts.
Note: Information is as of the end of 2020.
Source: ADB Cross-Border Settlement Infrastructure Forum (CSIF) Survey.

3. Distribution Channel

CIS may be distributed to investors in Singapore by the following entities regulated by the Monetary Authority of Singapore:

(i) The holders of Capital Markets Services License for dealing in capital markets products (specifically CIS), asset management and/or venture capital CIS management and registered CIS management companies; and

(ii) Exempt entities for dealing in capital markets products (specifically CIS) and asset management (including banks licensed under the Banking Act).

For more information on these entities, you may wish to refer to https://eservices.mas.gov.sg/fid/institution.

CIS = collective investment scheme.
Note: Information is as of the end of 2020.
Source: ADB Cross-Border Settlement Infrastructure Forum (CSIF) Survey.

4.   *Issuance of Collective Investment Scheme Unit*

Service Coverage Description
When a retail investor subscribes to a CIS, he or she will receive a confirmation (and not a physical beneficiary certificate) of purchase from the asset manager or the distributor. Then, his or her holdings will be entered into the register of participants under his/her name or the distributor's nominee account. Under the Securities and Futures (Offers of Investments) (Collective Investment Schemes) Regulations 2005 and the Variable Capital Companies Act, approved trustees of unit trusts and VCCs are, respectively, required to keep and maintain a register of members

CIS = collective investment scheme , VCC = variable capital company.
Note: Information is as of the end of 2020.
Source: ADB Cross-Border Settlement Infrastructure Forum (CSIF) Survey.

5.   *Cross-Border Collective Investment Scheme Transactions*

Home-Domiciled Collective Investment Scheme Sold Abroad (Outbound) Yes or No?	Foreign Collective Investment Schemes Sold in Your Economy (Inbound)		
	Yes or No	Data	Pertinent Laws
Yes	Yes	7,400 CIS	Securities and Futures Act (SFA)

CIS = collective investment scheme.
Note: Information is as of the end of 2020.
Source: ADB Cross-Border Settlement Infrastructure Forum (CSIF) Survey.

6.   *Central Platforms in Singapore*

Name of Central Platform	Operator	Model	ICSD Linkage
		TA Model	

ICSD = international central securities depository, TA = transfer agent.
Source: ADB Cross-Border Settlement Infrastructure Forum (CSIF) Survey.

Generally, CIS products are distributed through banks, insurance companies, securities firms, financial planning advisors, and other financial institutions licensed by the Monetary Authority of Singapore to distribute the products. There is no central platform in Singapore. Figure A1.10 demonstrates the post-trade process for the subscription and redemption of unlisted CIS units.

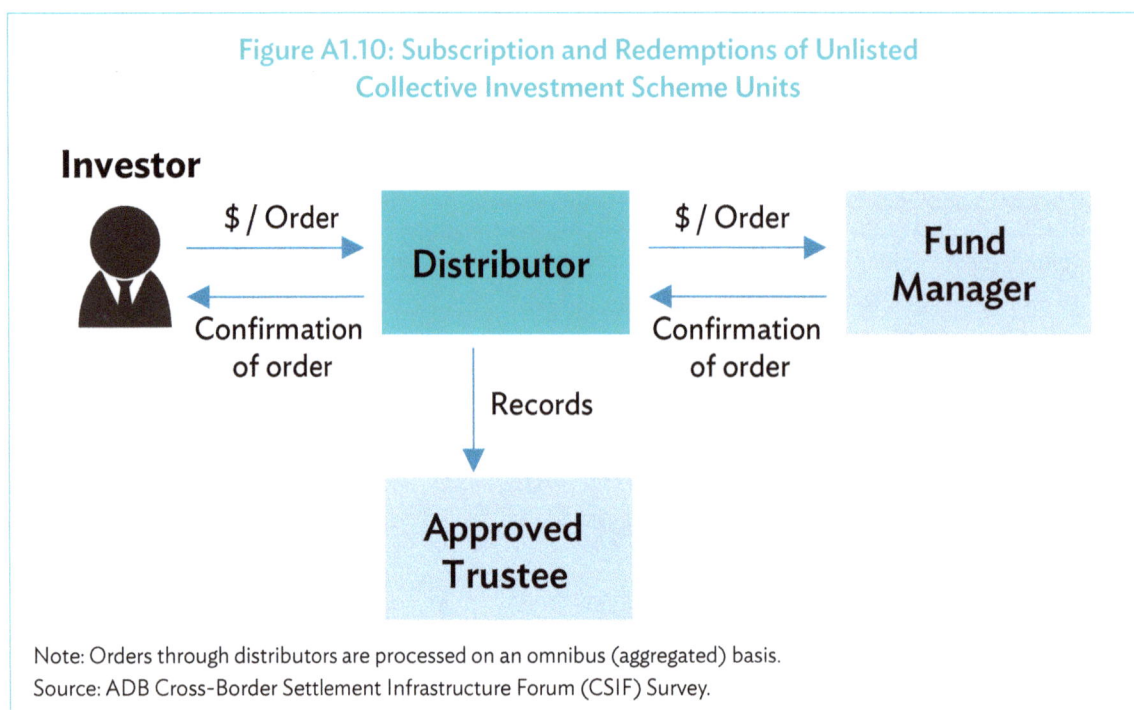

Figure A1.10: Subscription and Redemptions of Unlisted Collective Investment Scheme Units

Note: Orders through distributors are processed on an omnibus (aggregated) basis.
Source: ADB Cross-Border Settlement Infrastructure Forum (CSIF) Survey.

Figure A1.11 describes the post-trade process for the subscription and redemption of listed CIS units.

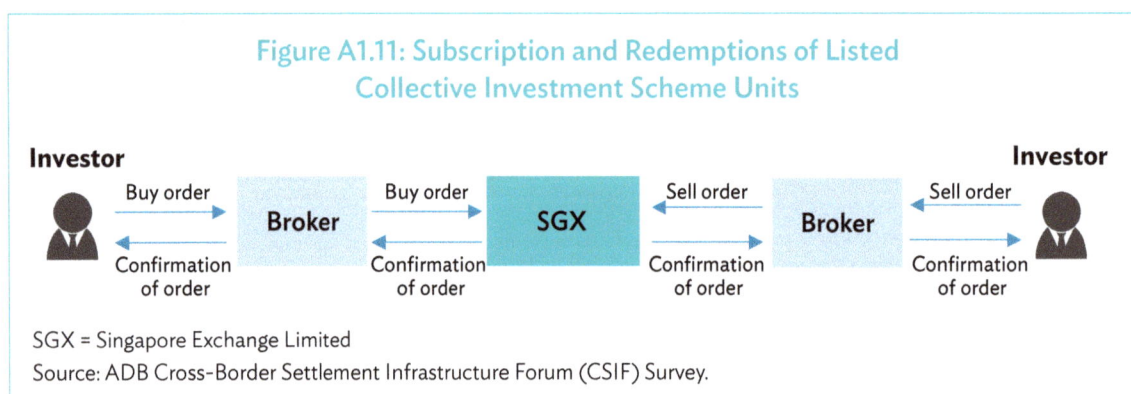

Figure A1.11: Subscription and Redemptions of Listed Collective Investment Scheme Units

SGX = Singapore Exchange Limited
Source: ADB Cross-Border Settlement Infrastructure Forum (CSIF) Survey.

7. Collective Investment Scheme Settlement of Subscription and Redemption

The issuance and redemption of the CIS units are done by the administrators, which also maintain the record of the unit holders. CIS records and holdings are neither deposited nor centralized with the CSD.

Therefore, subscription or redemption orders are not settled in a DVP manner in Singapore since the Singapore Exchange does not handle CIS-related post-trade processing.

L.   Thailand

1.   Market Size

AUM (A)	GDP (G)	A/G (%)	No. of CIS	Note
THB158.04 billion	THB494.59 billion	32	1,616	

AUM = assets under management, CIS = collective investment scheme, GDP = gross domestic product, THB = Thai baht.
Note: Information is as of the end of 2020.
Source: ADB Cross-Border Settlement Infrastructure Forum (CSIF) Survey.

2.   Legal Structure of Collective Investment Scheme

Collective Investment Scheme Type	Open-end vs. Closed-end	Redeemable vs. Traded on Exchange	Investment Company vs. Unincorporated	Market Share (%)
Mutual Fund	Open-end	Redeemable	Contractual CIS	85.78
Property CIS and REITs	Closed-end	Trade on exchange	Contractual CIS and Trust	7.38
Infrastructure CIS	Closed-end	Trade on exchange	Contractual CIS	6.48
ETF	Closed-end	Trade on exchange	Contractual CIS	0.37

CIS = collective investment scheme, ETF = exchange-traded fund, REITs = real estate investment trusts.
Note: Information is as of the end of 2020.
Source: ADB Cross-Border Settlement Infrastructure Forum (CSIF) Survey.

3.   Distribution Channel

	Distribution Channel				Electronic Platform Available?
Bank	Securities Company	Insurance Company		Others	
Yes	Yes	Yes		AMCs, Mutual Fund Brokerage, Securities Companies	Yes

AMC = asset management company.
Note: Information is as of the end of 2020.
Source: ADB Cross-Border Settlement Infrastructure Forum (CSIF) Survey.

4.   Issuance of Collective Investment Scheme Unit

Service Coverage	Description
△	Usually, registrars of CIS do not issue any certificates (electronic or physical) although they do provide holding statements. If needed, physical certificates can be issued by a CIS registrar upon the request of investor. Unless traded on the exchange, CIS units are not subjected to mandatory deposit at a CSD.

CIS = collective investment scheme, CSD = central securities depository.
Note: Information is as of the end of 2020.
Source: ADB Cross-Border Settlement Infrastructure Forum (CSIF) Survey.

5.   Cross-Border Collective Investment Scheme Transactions

Home-Domiciled Collective Investment Scheme Sold Abroad (Outbound) Yes or No?	Foreign Collective Investment Schemes Sold in Your Economy (Inbound)	
	Yes or No	**Pertinent Laws**
Yes	No	The act of direct marketing or soliciting by a foreign CIS is not permitted in Thailand. However, trades are possible via platform connectivity between TSD and Clearstream (FundConnext-Vestima linkage), for instance. Although it may depend on foreign economy regulations, the regulations in Thailand prescribe that the CIS has to specify where it is being sold (other than its home market).

CIS = collective investment scheme, TSD = Thailand Securities Depository.
Note: Information is as of the end of 2020.
Source: ADB Cross-Border Settlement Infrastructure Forum (CSIF) Survey.

6.   Central Platforms in Thailand

Name of Central Platform	Operator	Model	ICSD Linkage
FundConnext	SET	CSD Model	Clearstream

CSD = central securities depository, ICSD = international central securities depository, SET = Stock Exchange of Thailand.
Note: Information is as of the end of 2020.
Source: ADB Cross-Border Settlement Infrastructure Forum (CSIF) Survey.

As an infrastructure for CIS subscription and redemption in Thailand, FundConnext was developed under the leadership of the Stock Exchange of Thailand and went live in March 2017.

FundConnext serves as the digital gateway for the local capital market and consists of the functions described in Figures A1.12. and A1.13. FundConnext permits all transaction of the CIS onboarded at Clearstream, whether European, US, or from any other economy.

7.   Collective Investment Scheme Settlement of Subscription and Redemption

There is no DVP settlement case at the moment. CIS settlement in Thailand is done by commercial banks. Market participants may choose to use real-time gross settlement (RTGS) or not.

In Thailand, CIS units are not kept at a depository. The records of unitholders are maintained at a registrar and/or transfer agent. Therefore, settlement completeness is deemed final in the registrar and/or transfer agent records.

Figure A1.12: Digital Infrastructure in Thailand

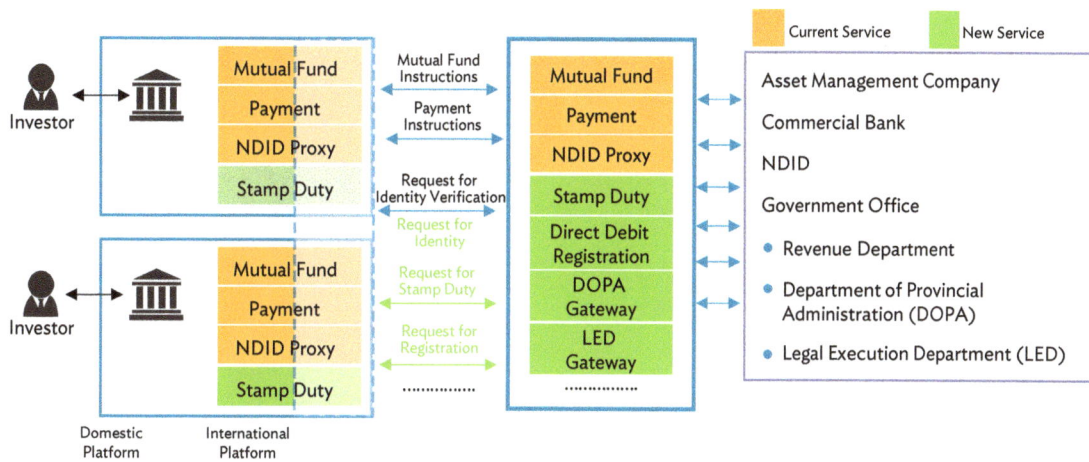

NDID = National Digital ID Company Limited.
Source: Asia Fund Standardization Forum (AFSF). 2019. Digital Infrastructure in Thailand. Bangkok.

Figure A1.13: Global Connectivity with ISO 20022 Standard of FundConnext

AMC = asset management company.
Source: Asia Fund Standardization Forum (AFSF). 2019. Digital Infrastructure in Thailand. Bangkok.

M.   Viet Nam

1.   Market Size of Collective Investment Scheme

AUM (A)	GDP (G)	A/G (%)	No. of CIS	Note
NA	343		40	ETFs (7), Closed-end CIS (3), Open-end CIS (30)
				(Only VSD statistics were reflected: No. of CIS includes only funds using VSD services. Other funds have not used VSD services, thus, details remain unknown and VSD does not have data.)

AUM = assets under management, CIS = collective investment scheme, ETF = exchange-traded fund, GDP = gross domestic product, NA = not applicable, VSD = Vietnam Securities Depository.
Note: Information is as of the end of 2020.
Source: ADB Cross-Border Settlement Infrastructure Forum (CSIF) Survey.

2.   Legal Structure of Collective Investment Scheme

Collective Investment Scheme Type	Open-end vs. Closed-end	Redeemable vs. Traded on Exchange	Investment Company vs. Unincorporated	Market Share (%)
ETF	Open-end	Trade on exchange	NA	NA
Open-end	Open-end	Redeemable	NA	NA
Closed-end	Closed-end	Trade on exchange	NA	NA

ETF = exchange-traded fund, NA = not applicable.
Notes:
1. Vietnam Securities Depository (VSD) acts as the transfer agent and does not calculate the net asset value (NAV) of collective investment scheme (CIS). Therefore, VSD is unable to provide statistical data regarding asset under management and market share.
2. Information is as of the end of 2020.
Source: ADB Cross-Border Settlement Infrastructure Forum (CSIF) Survey.

3.   Distribution Channel

Distribution Channel				Electronic Platform Available?
Bank	Securities Company	Insurance Company	Others	
		NA		

Note: Information is as of the end of 2020.
Source: ADB Cross-Border Settlement Infrastructure Forum (CSIF) Survey.

4.   *Issuance of Collective Investment Scheme Unit*

Service Coverage	Description
△	– For ETFs, with the characteristic of being listed on the exchange, VSD uses the electronic registration. – For open-end CIS, VSD is the transfer agent and electronic registration is applied. – For closed-end CIS, units can be either issued in physical certificate or electronically registered, depending on the status of deposit.

CIS = collective investment scheme, ETF = exchange-traded fund, VSD = Vietnam Securities Depository.
Note: Information is as of the end of 2020.
Source: ADB Cross-Border Settlement Infrastructure Forum (CSIF) Survey.

5.   *Cross-Border Collective Investment Scheme Transactions*

Home-Domiciled Collective Investment Scheme Sold Abroad (Outbound) Yes or No?	Foreign Collective Investment Schemes Sold in Your Economy (Inbound)		
	Yes or No	Data	Pertinent Laws
No	No		

Note: Information is as of the end of 2020.
Source: ADB Cross-Border Settlement Infrastructure Forum (CSIF) Survey.

6.   *Central Platforms in Viet Nam*

Name of Central Platform	Operator	Model	ICSD Linkage
Open-ended Fund Management System and ETFs System	VSD	CSD Model	

CSD = central securities depository, ETF = exchange-traded fund, ICSD = international central securities depository, VSD = Vietnam Securities Depository.
Note: Information is as of the end of 2020.
Source: ADB Cross-Border Settlement Infrastructure Forum (CSIF) Survey.

Viet Nam has developed and operated a management system for the subscription and redemption of public CIS described in Figure A1.14.

Figure A1.14: Initial Public Offering of Open-End Collective Investment Schemes in Viet Nam

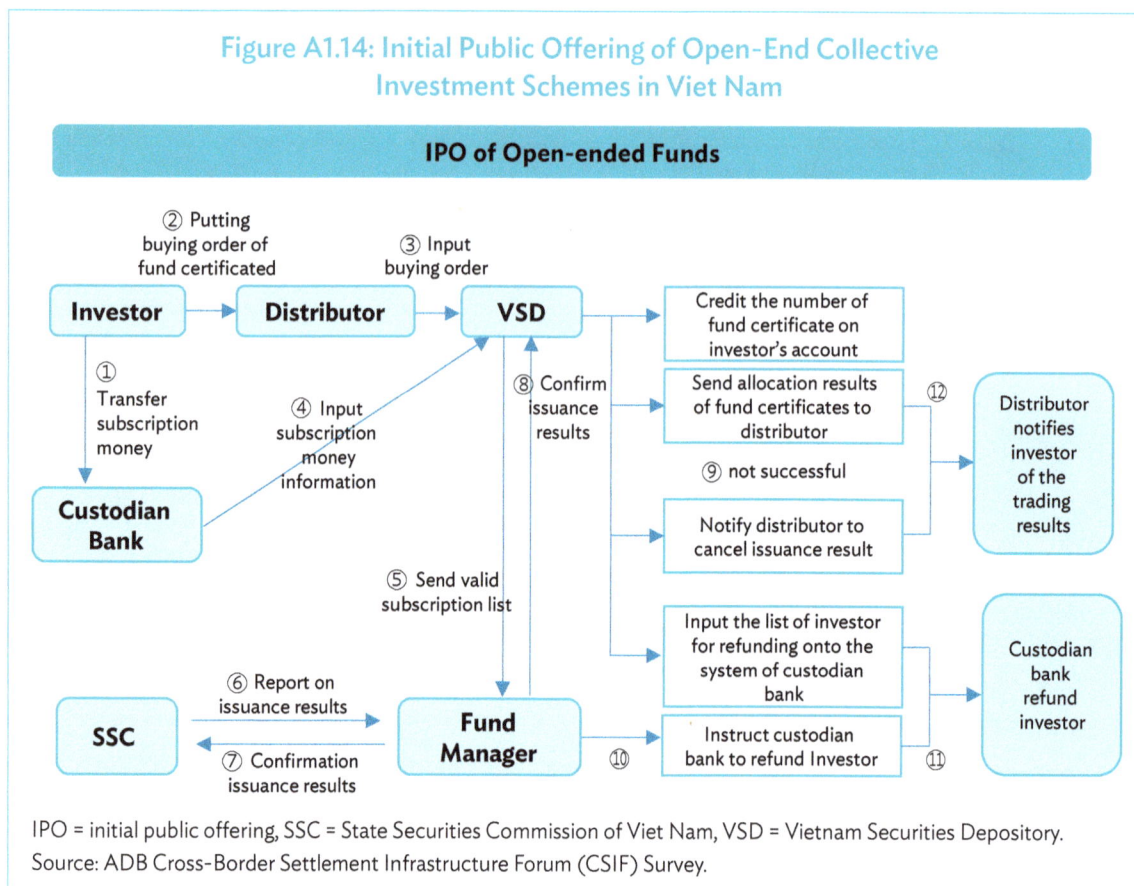

IPO = initial public offering, SSC = State Securities Commission of Viet Nam, VSD = Vietnam Securities Depository.
Source: ADB Cross-Border Settlement Infrastructure Forum (CSIF) Survey.

7.   *CIS Settlement Model and Completeness and Finality of Settlement*

Settlement of Subscription and Redemption
DVP settlement is applied to secondary trading of exchange-traded funds (ETFs) on the exchange. For the subscription and redemption of ETFs on the primary market, DVP is not applied. Investors need to hand in the money before clearing is activated.

Legal Requirements on settlement completeness
Viet Nam does stipulate the cut-off time of settlement completion.

For the legal requirements of settlement completeness relating to CIS products, the reference should be Circular 119/2020/TT-BTC, as the settlement of ETFs on a subscription and/or redemption will relate to an ownership transfer of the underlying stocks in the index basket, detailed definition of such transfer is regulated in Article 6. Paragraph (i).

Box A1.6: Legal Requirements on Settlement Completeness

(Circular 119/2020/TT-BTC)

Article 6. Transfer of ownership of securities

1. The transfer of ownership of securities centrally registered with VSD shall be carried out by VSD according to the following principles:

    a) Transfer of ownership of securities through securities transactions conducted through the securities trading system;

    b) Transfer of ownership of securities outside the securities trading systems if such transfers are non-commercial in nature or fail to be executed via the securities trading system.

2. Cases of transfer of ownership of securities as prescribed in point b clause 1 hereof include:

    (…)

    i) Transfer of ownership of structure securities, fund certificates in swap transactions with the exchange-traded fund (ETF) (…)

    The "**swap transactions**" mentioned herein are the subscription and redemption of ETFs on the primary market, it is not the secondary trading on the Exchange.

(Circular 98/2020/TT-BTC_ The most important legal reference)

Article 2

10. "fund certificate trading day" means the day on which the fund management company, on behalf of the fund, creates and redeems fund certificates or creation units from authorized participants/investors according to the fund's trading mechanism.

VSD = Vietnam Securities Depository.
Source: ADB Cross-Border Settlement Infrastructure Forum (CSIF) Survey.

Please refer to Box A1.7.

Box A1.7: Schedule of Clearance and Settlement for Stocks and Fund Certificates Traded on Stock Exchange of Guideline on Securities Clearing and Settlement (Decision 211/QD-VSD, Dated 18 December 2015, issued by CEO of VSD)

Relating to the cycle of subscription and redemption of CIS between investors and Funds. The cycle of subscription and redemption of ETFs is (T+1) day, with T day being the day when investors send in orders and T+1 being the settlement day. As for this primary trading of ETFs, the T day (trading day) is only for receipt of investors orders. On T+1, investors can cancel their orders if they do not wish for a subscription/redemption by sending Written Notice with Approval of Funds Management Companies to VSD before the time of clearing and settlement, which happens in the afternoon. Otherwise, in case they want to proceed, they will hand in money through banks within T+1 and their stocks will be cut off for clearing and settlement purposes around 16:00 o'clock, then they will receive ETFs which they subscribe for at the end of T+1 (normally 17:00 o'clock, after the system runs thoroughly). As for a sell order of ETFs, the same cut off time will be applied around 16:00 o'clock on T+1 day, investors will receive the underlying stocks and money on T+1. In case they do not want to proceed the orders, they need to notify VSD as soon as possible with a Written Notice approved by Funds Management Companies before the settlement time.

CIS = collective investment scheme, ETF = exchange-traded fund, VSD = Vietnam Securities Depository.
Source: ADB Cross-Border Settlement Infrastructure Forum (CSIF) Survey.

Reference can be found in the regulation on ETF registration, depository, clearing and settlement, and right exercises to be issued by Vietnam Securities Depository along with Decision No. 46/QD-VSD dated 8 April 2021.

Legal Requirements on Settlement Finality and Irrevocability

Article 37, Clause 1 of Circular 119/2020/TT-BTC stipulates the cases that allow settlement removal, as follows:

- ▶ Clearing members and customers of clearing members sell securities that are not in their ownership in accordance with the guidance of the Ministry of Finance;

- ▶ Transactions of clearing members or customers of clearing members are carried out after Vietnam Securities Depository notifies Viet Nam Stock Exchange of the suspension of operations of that clearing member;

- ▶ Transactions conducted for securities codes that have not been accepted for clearing and settlement on the system of Vietnam Securities Depository;

- ▶ The transaction has an invalid account number because the clearing member registration number or the trading account type character does not exist;

- ▶ The transaction contains invalid information, including no session code; trading date is different from the current one; there is no buying or selling order number; price, trading volume is less than or equal to zero; no order confirmation;

- ▶ The transaction has a combination of four information such as market code, trading board code, security code, and order confirmation number, which are identical with the previously received transaction; and

- ▶ Other cases after being approved by the State Securities Commission.

However, Article 37 of Circular 119 can only be applied to the case of secondary trading of ETFs on the exchange, with no relation to the subscription and redemption of ETFs. As for trading on the exchange with T+2 settlement cycle (secondary trading) of ETF, it is up to the DVP settlement method, so there could be a failure in the settlement if there is a shortage of money or securities at the time the settlement is handled.

For primary trading relating to subscription and redemption of ETFs, there is no DVP applied at the time of the settlement, investors always have to hand in the cash before clearing is activated, so there should be no case of failure, instead, a finality is always ensured.

On the settlement cycle of CIS trading on secondary market (on the stock exchange), which is (T+2) days, it is still applicable and unchanged. As of 16:00 on T+2, VSD members receive money and securities according to netted result.

Article 43 of Circular 98/2020/TT-BTC presents in detail the regulations of primary subscription and redemption of ETF.

GLOSSARY

accounting date	The end of a collective investment scheme's (CIS) (fund) accounting period, for which the income accrued during that period may subsequently be distributed to investors.
acknowledgement	A message returned by the fund-side institution to the client-side institution, which indicates that an order has been received and accepted for execution.
administrator	An entity that carries out the administration functions for a CIS (fund) or CIS (fund) management company, including the CIS (fund) management company itself and transfer agent, as appropriate.
aggregator	A client-side institution that maintains a single holding in a CIS (fund) on behalf of multiple clients, from whom it receives orders to deal and passes them to the fund-side institution as a single consolidated order (e.g., fund supermarkets). (See also platform.)
Ancillary System Interface	In TARGET2, all ancillary systems (e.g., securities settlement, individual, and retail payment systems) can settle transactions directly in central bank money. As a matter of principle, payments can be settled on any real-time gross settlement (RTGS) account. Ancillary systems can take advantage of standardized access and clearing procedures.
CIS (fund) provider	The CIS (fund) management company.
CIS (fund) units	The participating shares or units in an investment CIS (fund)
client-side institution	A financial institution that represents or provides services to the underlying investor in the order and settlement process, including fund supermarkets and other distributors, as well as client custodians.
closed-end fund	Fund launched through an initial public offering (IPO) in order to raise money and only issues a fixed amount of units. (See also open-end fund.)
commission	Remuneration paid to a distributor by the CIS (fund) sponsor in connection with subscription orders and the continued holding of the units concerned.
confirmation	A message returned by the CIS (fund)-side institution to the client-side institution, which confirms the full details of an order that has been executed.
cross-border	Activities connected to the distribution of funds in countries other than their home domiciles.

CSD	An entity that holds securities and other assets in order that domestic transactions may be effected for beneficial owners and settled by way of entries within its own books.
CSD link	A link for securities settlement between an investor central securities depository (CSD) and a technical issuer CSD must be opened among CSDs before any cross-CSD transaction can be settled. Each CSD link is manifested by a CSD omnibus account and a CSD mirror account (TARGET2-Securities [T2S] term).
CSD participant	Participant of a CSD, including banks, financial institutions, central counterparties (CCPs), stock exchanges, multilateral trade platforms, and CSDs and clearing banks; CSD participants have account(s) at the CSD and use these accounts for securities transactions and safekeeping.
custodian	Safekeeps securities and manages cash for its clients (e.g., investors, distributors, asset managers, and other custodians).
DCA	Dedicated cash account; all cash bookings in T2S are settled on sub-accounts of RTGS accounts. Each securities account has one and only one DCA, but one DCA can be used. Balances do not remain on the DCAs overnight.
deal (marking)	Mechanism for identifying each distributor to whom the order relates.
depositary	Financial institution that is appointed under a CIS' (fund's) constitution to oversee the operation of the fund and to whom its assets are entrusted for safekeeping.
depository	See CSD.
distribution channel	CIS (fund) products can reach investors through a diverse range of distribution channels such as banks, securities companies, or insurance companies. Apart from these conventional face-to-face channels, which still play a dominant role in Asia, dependence on screen-based electronic platform is growing amid the trend of squeezing middle margins and lowering costs.
distribution units	CIS (fund) units, the income accruing to which is distributed to investors following the end of the accounting period.
distributor	A client-side institution that promotes to its customers the sale of units issued by CIS (funds) of one or more CIS (fund) provider and acts as the client's agent in the order input/placement process.
DVP or RVP	Delivery versus payment or receive versus payment is a simultaneous exchange of securities against cash.
euro	The currency of the euro area, it is spelled in lower case and is a collective noun (i.e., "euros" as a plural form is incorrect).

euro area	The collective of European Union member states that have adopted the euro as their sole official currency.
Eurosystem	The monetary authority of the euro area. The Eurosystem is a subset of the European System of Central Banks that consists of the European Central Bank and the national central banks of the European Union member states that belong to the euro area.
exchange-traded fund (ETF)	An ETF is a type of security that tracks an index, sector, commodity, or other asset, but which can be purchased or sold on a stock exchange the same way as a regular stock.
execution	The processing of an order by the CIS-(fund)-side institution through the fund's or its own books.
investment company	An investment company is a corporation or trust engaged in the business of investing the pooled capital of investors in financial securities. This is most often done either through a closed-end fund or an open-end fund.
investor CSD	A CSD that holds a security for which it is not the/an issuer CSD; it holds these securities either directly or indirectly via one or more intermediaries at the issuer CSD.
issuer CSD	A CSD in which securities are issued (or immobilized). The issuer CSD opens accounts allowing investors (in a direct holding system) and/or intermediaries (including investor CSDs) to hold these securities.
issuing agent	The agent appointed by the fund to manage the issuance process and the creation or cancellation of fund shares in the fund issuance account.
mutual fund	A mutual fund commonly found in the US can be explained as an open-end fund that is redeemable, and in the form of an investment company. (See also unit trust.)
open-end fund	There are no restriction on the amount of units the CIS (fund) can issue. When an investor purchases a fund, more units are simply created. (See also closed-end fund.)
order	A transaction to invest in or sell units in an investment fund. (See also subscription and redemption.)
order giver	The originator or sender of an investment funds order (subscription, redemption, or switch).
order routing	The automated handling of subscriptions and redemptions of units or shares of a CIS (fund), which uses an order routing mechanism that connects and automates the trading, reporting, settlement, and payment processes; it gives fund managers, transfer agents, and distributors/platforms a real time view of the status of all their domestic and global fund trades, payment status, and liquidity requirements.

payment bank	The owner of an RTGS account and its associated DCAs is called a payment bank in T2S. The quality of cash held by a payment bank on its account at a national central bank is central bank money.
platform	A client-side institution that aggregates orders from multiple clients and places them with the relevant fund-side institution. (See also aggregator.)
PM account	Payment module (PM) account means an account held by a TARGET2 participant in the PM with a central bank, which is necessary for such TARGET2 participant to (i) submit payment orders or receive payments via TARGET2, and (ii) settle payment with such a central bank.
Prop FTP	Prop FTP stands for Proprietary Format File Transfer Protocol. A proprietary format is a file format of a company, organization, or individual that contains data that is ordered and stored according to a particular encoding-scheme, designed by the company or organization to be secret, such that the decoding and interpretation of this stored data is easily accomplished only with particular software or hardware that the company itself has developed. The specification of the data encoding format is not released, or underlies non-disclosure agreements.
PTP instruction	This is used as one of the terms to describe S-INVEST, Indonesia's order routing infrastructure. PTP instruction is for trade allocation and trade details, trade confirmation, settlement instruction, and over-the-counter instruction creation.
redeemable	Investors sell a fund by requesting the distributor to redeem their fund, and receive the according amount of return that is derived from the fund net asset value. (See also traded on exchange.)
redemption	A transaction whereby units in a CIS (fund) are sold back to the CIS (fund) or CIS (fund) management company. (See also order.)
register	Official record of holders of a CIS (fund).
RTGS account	A real-time gross settlement account is a cash account for central bank money settlement in TARGET2.
settlement	The process of transferring the cash value of a transaction to or from the CIS (fund) or CIS (fund) management company in exchange for the registration or deregistration (as appropriate) of title to the units concerned, may be effected by actual movements between the client-side and CIS (fund) administrator or via a CSD/international central securities depository (ICSD).
subscription	A transaction whereby units in a CIS (fund) are purchased from the CIS (fund) or CIS (fund) management company. (See also order.)
T2S	TARGET2-Securities (T2S) is a European securities settlement engine, which aims to offer centralized DVP settlement in central bank money across all European securities markets. It is owned and operated by the Eurosystem.

TARGET	Trans-European Automated Real-Time Gross Settlement Express Transfer is a system for central bank payments execution that has been replaced by T2.
technical issuer	The CSD where the CSD omnibus account of an investor CSD is opened is the technical issuer CSD for a security held by the participants of the investor CSD. The term is appropriate for a CSD that performs issuance of a subset of the global issued position of a security (issuer CSD).
traded on exchange	Investors sell fund by trading it on the stock exchange, and wait for a buy order from another investor, which will be set based on market price. (See also redeemable.)
transfer	The movement of units between two accounts recorded in the legal register of fund holders; this may occur between different holders or between two accounts of the same holder.
transfer agent	A CIS (fund)-side institution in many jurisdictions that executes the issue and redemption of units on the CIS's (fund) behalf and usually maintains the register of title.
unincorporated	Unincorporated (mutual fund) means any partnership, each partner of which is a corporation, engaged solely in the business of investing and reinvesting funds in investments, or holding or selling investments for the purpose of realizing income or profit.
unit trust	A unit trust from the United Kingdom will be an open-end fund that is redeemable, but unincorporated. (See also mutual fund.)